EDWARD R. MURROW
THE WAR YEARS

by

R. Franklin Smith

UPSALA COLLEGE LIBRARY
WIRTHS CAMPUS

Dedicated to:

Those CBS and BBC Wartime Colleagues of Ed Murrow
Who remember him well

"Like thousands of others here who remember the war years, those years always bring you back to our minds. We were a bit short on friends in those days, Ed, we weren't a very good risk by any means. In the first half of this game, we were being hammered--our supporters had gone--nations stood around like a crowd round an execution--waiting for us to get the 'chop.' You didn't, though, did you? You steamed up and down that touch line yelling your head off . . . .

"Now the tumult has died--the crowds have gone--the dead are buried--the arena is empty.

"I'm just an ordinary, working bloke--nothing special, but I remember you--and the friendly voice in the air that reached us in the days that seem as just 'yesterday.'"

                    To Edward R. Murrow

                    From R. H. Hodkinson
                    Middleton, Manchester
                    England

                    17 March 1965

4604

CONTENTS

PREFACE v

CHAPTER

I. RADIO'S MISSION: A YOUTHFUL EDWARD R. MURROW EXPOUNDS HIS BROADCAST PHILOSOPHY 7

II. FIRST IMPRESSIONS: A SIZING UP 15

III. ON THE JOB: WAR COMES TO AN ADJUSTING BBC 21

IV. ED MURROW AS BROADCASTER, MODERATOR, AND ADMINISTRATOR: AN EVALUATION BY HIS WARTIME COLLEAGUES . 28

V. THE BBC MILIEU AND INFLUENCE 49

VI. A PHILOSOPHY OF REPORTING 56

VII. REPORTING: RADIO, TV, AND INTERVIEWING---SOME SPECIFICS 73

VIII. ARTIST AT THE MICROPHONE 83

IX. ARTIST OF ORAL LANGUAGE 91

X. ARTIST WITHOUT PEER 95

XI. THE DOUGHTY ANGLOPHILE 99

XII. WARTIME SERVICE 106

XIII. RECOGNITION 111

XIV. THE "OBJECTIVE" REPORTER 115

XV. UNHAPPY EXECUTIVE 128

XVI. "HE GRIPPED PEOPLE" 135

XVII. "THIS I BELIEVE" 139

SELECTED READINGS 149

APPENDIX A---INTERVIEWS 150

PREFACE

In the spring of 1973, a major draft of this book was completed by Dr. R. Franklin (Bob) Smith, Associate Professor of Communications Arts and Sciences, Western Michigan University. In May of that year, he and his wife set off for a three-week return visit to England to renew his contacts and continue his research so that the book might be brought to fulfillment. One week after his return home, he died suddenly and without warning. In the aftermath of the bereavement, his wife Nancy turned the manuscript over to two of his friends for criticism. One was a colleague at the University, Dr. Jules Rossman, the other, the music critic for the *Kalamazoo Gazette*, Diane Heintz. Without their enthusiastic support, as well as initial criticism, all hope of posthumous publication might have ceased. The author would be pleased with their contribution.

The remainder of this Preface is essentially as Dr. Smith wrote it.

Edward R. Murrow died at his home in Pawling, New York, in April of 1965.

At this time, a new theory on the role of mass media expounded by a Canadian professor was the talk of Academia. Marshall McLuhan proclaimed the age of the electronic "turn on" and "tune in," the age of instantness and, now, of light and visual impressions. The ancient and literate departmental modes of meaning and thinking are now over, said the professor. We are all part of a tribal village, "as small as the town square, as large as the planet." We will be "roughed up" in the process of adjustment, as we are subconsciously "massaged" by the new media. And the message, the only message, is the technology itself.

Perhaps the mid-1960's were a transitional phase between a "new" and "old" order of communication environment. The 1970's certainly have continued the "roughing up" process of which McLuhan spoke. But in this book we are attempting to take a journey back---in time and in technology---to that period when the media were in their infancy, just beginning to influence publics and affect the decisions of leaders and nations.

The reporting of news by electronic media in the United States, in a very real sense, began with Edward R. Murrow. True, during the 1920's and 1930's, there was some commentary and some news, rigid but weak, controlled by a Press-Radio Bureau. News by radio often was not broadcast until after the newspapers had come out.

But a war, and Ed Murrow, and his many colleagues, came along. It was Murrow's effort that contributed much to the regular and systematic reporting of events---currently and often from on-the-spot---by radio, and later by television. And McLuhan does have his point. No matter how many read papers, and certainly millions do, millions more listen to and watch the electronic news media. Theory and mysticism aside, it is simply more direct and easier for most individuals to regard the world through the ear and moving pictures than by scanning the cold printed page.

This book, then, is about a man and his work. It is an attempt to find out who Edward R. Murrow was at the time he evolved as a young reporter and news analyst in England during the World War II era. What was his professional role? How was he able to help lift up British spirits at one of the darkest periods in their modern history? Why was he acclaimed as a great journalist and broadcaster? What did he contribute to our understanding of news reporting and commentary? Of the nature of broadcast journalism? What do his life and work say to us today in our concern with the media's view of the world? These are questions for which this book seeks to provide some answers---tentative as they may be.

Edward R. Murrow was the CBS European Director from 1937 through 1946. His headquarters was London. He lived and worked there for nine years. This is the period under examination here. References to his life before or after this period are included only insofar as they may relate to his work and character. The "Murrow of London" story is told essentially through oral and written comments from people who worked with and knew Ed Murrow during these critical years. These people were his professional associates in one way or another. BBC sound and film libraries and written archives also contributed much to the work.

The author owes a special debt of gratitude to the following, who contributed much to this book: Charles Curran, Director General, BBC; Noel Harvey, Head of Liaison, Overseas & Foreign Relations, BBC; Mary Hodgeson, Written Archives Center, Caversham Park, BBC; R. D. Hewlett, Head of Reference & Registry Services, BBC; Mrs. B. J. Milnes, Granada TV Limited; Margaret Evling, The Royal Institute of International Affairs; Frank Gillard; Sir Lindsay Wellington; Tom Barman; Leonard Miall, Controller, Overseas & Foreign Relations, BBC; R. D. Marriott; Patrick Smith, Geneva; Romney Wheeler, Division of Public Relations, Consumers Power Company, Jackson, Michigan; Dennis Perry, Written Archives Center, Caversham Park; Mrs. Darsie Gillie, Mirabeau Vaucluse, France; E. Colston Shepherd; Herbert Agar; Eric Wavr; Royston Morley, TV Center, BBC; Pierre Lefevre; Howard Marshall; Maurice Gorlam, Dublin; Mrs. Rilta Valentine, Chevy Chase, Maryland; Mr. and Mrs. Michael Standing; Mrs. Mary Adams; Miss I. D. Benzie; Mr. and Mrs. Robert Reid; Robin Duff, Old Meldrum, Scotland; Robert Dunnett, Edinburgh; Kenneth Mathew; Cyril Ray; Godfrey Talbot; Robert Barr; Michael Balkwill; D. G. Bridson; Charles Collingwood, CBS News; Eric Sevareid, CBS News; Mr. and Mrs. Ronald Pattison, at Dorking, Surrey; Mrs. Eleanor Horan, Administrative Assistant, and Gregory Henderson, Director, Edward R. Murrow Center of Public Diplomacy, Tufts University, Medford, Massachusetts; the staff at BBC Written Archives, Caversham Park. Thanks are also owed to the Columbia Broadcasting System for providing the cover photo. Finally, it is with heartfelt thanks and appreciation that I wish to recognize the helpful contributions and continuing encouragement of Mrs. Edward R. Murrow.

CHAPTER I

RADIO'S MISSION: A YOUTHFUL EDWARD R. MURROW

EXPOUNDS HIS BROADCAST PHILOSOPHY

Crisp, cool air enveloped the English countryside. Yet when the sun shone, as it will do even in an English spring, it shed warmth; so another May had arrived, and the long British spring was yielding its harvest of azaleas and roses. There was also excitement in the air. For the Empire was to have a new king, ascending to the throne under circumstances never experienced before. The hereditary claimant, Edward VIII, had abdicated "to marry the woman I love." His brother, soon to be crowned, would be George VI.
A train slowly settled to a stop at London's Waterloo Station. It had come from the south coast with its party of travelers from New York. A young man stood nervously waiting in the station for his guest, his assignment to welcome the new man to his post. Richard Marriott, Foreign Liaison Officer for the BBC, recalls that he had no idea what the American visitor looked like, and worried about what he would say after he had shaken his hand, welcomed him to England, and wished him happiness in his new job.
The ceremony turned out to be brief and pleasant. The 29-year-old newly appointed CBS European Director seemed to know what he was to do. Marriott saw him to a taxi and he slipped away from the station, presumably to his Queen Anne's Street flat. Edward R. Murrow had arrived in London. Except for brief visits back home, he would remain there for a decade, throughout the war years. It was March, 1937. Not until the Spring of 1946 would he return to America, world famous and a major executive of the Columbia Broadcasting System.
Murrow's position was that of representative of his network in England. In that capacity his job would be to administer the London office and supervise the arrangement of broadcasts, as his predecessors had done. But something new was soon to be added. As Mariott summed it up,

> Before, both Cesar Searchinger [Murrow's predecessor] and Fred Bate [NBC] were arrangers; they ran the office, they were the representatives of their companies. Their job was to find speakers to talk about things. They had wonderful contacts. Fred Bate knew everybody---was a friend of the Prince of Wales. He moved in useful circles. And Cesar Searchinger was a very good operator. They didn't broadcast, themselves. Ed was something new. He did most of the broadcasting, as well as being representative.[1]

---

[1]These and most other quoted materials in the book are taken from the verbatim record of a series of interviews conducted by

The Foreign Department of the BBC was the official contact for Murrow, and if CBS wanted anything done it was the Foreign Department Murrow consulted. Marriott's office was responsible for seeing that their outside broadcasts, their lines and the facilities required were provided. Nothing was recorded, and it was a case of first come, first served. Marriott remembers that CBS and NBC never wanted to share facilities.

Still, the competition between the two networks was not a personal feud between their two representatives. While Marriott sensed a certain tension and acidity between Cesar Searchinger and Fred Bate, he was convinced that Bate and Murrow liked each other personally. Being liked was a habit with the young CBS director, a quality of character that would reach out to attract colleagues, competitors, leaders, and the average Briton alike.

During those last placid months before Britain's long wartime ordeal began, Murrow's task was to cover events of all kinds, including the Davis Cup and Wimbledon matches. There would be nothing highly formal or academic in Murrow's approach to broadcasting events, much to the chagrin of the late Sir John Reith, the noted BBC Director General whose views initially fixed the BBC's philosophy of broadcasting and are still reflected in its programming.

Shortly after his arrival at his new post, Murrow was granted an interview with that top executive. The imposing and powerful figure paid him the supreme compliment of stating that "in view of your record, I daresay your company's programs in the future will be a little more intellectual." "On the contrary," was Murrow's answer, and he thereupon proceeded to present his concept of the role of this revolutionary instrument of communication. It would not be a medium for academics, but for everyone. "I want our programs to be anything but intellectual," commented Murrow. "I want them to be down to earth, in the vernacular of the man on the street."

"Hmph!" grunted Sir John. "Then you will drag radio down to the level of the Hyde Park Speakers' Corner." "Exactly, and

---

the author. Persons interviewed, the dates of these interviews, and other pertinent information concerning them can be found in the Interview Schedule located in Appendix A. Consequently, footnotes will be used in this book only when necessary to provide citations for sources other than these interviews, and occasionally to provide explanatory data that does not fit neatly into the text but may be helpful to the reader. The reader is urged to become familiar with the "cast of characters" set forth in the Interview Schedule since this will contribute toward a better understanding of Edward R. Murrow and his basic ideas concerning broadcast journalism. It is their many lucid comments about Ed Murrow that have made it possible for the author to develop the Murrow personality in its many facets as it relates to those eventful war years.

literally," Murrow shot back. "I also plan to broadcast from English pubs, from the Brighton Pier, and from crowded places on Bank Holidays. And, I plan to cover many sporting events in addition to the usual tennis matches."

Former BBC talks producer, Robert Dunnett, recalls the first time he met Murrow. It was at the beautiful St. Andrews golf links, and the event was the British Open Championship. The Scotsman remembers a "keen, lean young American" he met near the eighteenth fairway where there was a row of small buildings for the broadcasting and press facilities. Murrow presented an impression of polite efficiency. "There was an instant rapport" Dunnett recalled. "I recognized a professional when I saw one." This was a truly amazing first-impression evaluation by a professional man who had had no formal training in journalism and was barely in his first year as head of the British CBS operation. It was at this meeting that Murrow displayed an understanding and awareness that were soon to contribute to his memorable wartime broadcasts. He knew intuitively that radio was made for something beyond merely transmitting the human voice.

"I hear a pipe band," Murrow told Dunnett, as they stood near the building where a broadcaster would report the final exciting putts. "If we open the window, we can get the band in." A small example, but indicative of Murrow's belief that radio must transmit the real world with all of its trimmings and harshness to communicate fully with listeners. "He had the acuteness," Dunnett has noted, "to perceive the sound possibility inherent in the situation."

Just six months later, Ed Murrow would impress others, only this time from the public platform. On this occasion, Murrow presented a lecture entitled "The International Aspects of Broadcasting" at Chatham House under the sponsorship of the Royal Institute of International Affairs. Royston Morley, later a producer and director for BBC Television, recalls this occasion most favorably. Morley began his career with the BBC in television during the thirties, when TV made its first appearance in the world on British screens. Morley's wife, Miss I. D. Benzie, also attended but was not impressed. "He didn't know his subject. I could have done it better," the former Foreign Director of the BBC and Richard Marriott's boss during the thirties bluntly summed it up. In fact, Miss Benzie apparently was one of a very small minority who heard Murrow that day and did not relate positively to him and to his ideas. She later acidly recalled an evening in Paris with Murrow: "We had nothing to say to one another. He bored me." She disliked theatricality in people and she hinted that Ed Murrow had more than a "tinge" of histrionics in his character. "Does he want to become a star?" she asked. Repeatedly she declared that there was something "soft" about Murrow, "a kind of vulnerability," but without ever elaborating the specifics of her dislike. She conceded, however, that he presented her with no particular grief in his requests for facilities and help from her office.

Perhaps Murrow sensed her disdain. In 1937 he gave Royston Morley a Christmas present, a subscription to *The New Yorker*, his favorite magazine. The gift may have been prompted by a wish to ingratiate himself with the Morleys, or Murrow may simply have tried indicating his fondness for Morley. Whichever, it was typical of Murrow's generosity that characterized his dealings with his colleagues throughout his career.

The speech that Murrow delivered in the former home of William Pitt, Earl of Chatham, at Number 10 St. James Square, bears examination, despite Miss Benzie's reservations about it. But first a brief look at the speaker's background and qualifications is in order. Not yet thirty years of age, an executive of a major American broadcasting network, Ed Murrow was always more than willing to expound his philosophy of communications, the media, and the world.

It was not surprising that the Royal Institute invited him to speak. His position was of sufficient importance to warrant his appearance, but his background also gave him special qualifications. During his twenties, the young man from Washington state had traversed the Atlantic more than once and had become professionally engaged in and concerned about international affairs as Assistant Director of the Institute of International Education (IIE). An experienced debater and speaker, guided in college by an inspiring speech teacher, Ida Lou Anderson, Murrow was a student of history, having achieved a perspective through intensive study and thought that he would continue to hold and nurture throughout his broadcasting career.

Born in North Carolina, from a humble home, he had seen the land of America from there to the northwest. The youngest of three sons, he retained his pride in once having worked as a lumberjack. While working for the IIE, he developed an intense hatred of fascism, and in that position he helped German professors and scientists---one of them named Albert Einstein---to escape Hitler's tyranny.

To return to the 1937 Chatham House lecture, Murrow posed the basic questions of what is the basic role or purpose of broadcasting, and what are its international aspects? War was less than two years away and Munich, less than a year. In four months the Austrian *Anschluss* would take place, and Murrow would be in Vienna to make his first direct newscast from the scene of a major political event. And the electronic medium of radio---as later with television---would never again be quite the same.

Murrow read his Royal Institute speech on that November evening because, as he put it facetiously, "any American speaking to a British audience may be in need of an interpreter." But more seriously he warned, "I have no desire either to offend or to criticize without intent." And the subject was of such importance that it merited a careful choice of words.

At the outset he signaled the direction he would take, the tone he would adopt. It was to be challenging, critical, with a dash of warning pessimism. He first recalled researching his subject, finding that authors of that period seemed only to stress the "blessings of broadcasting." Most spoke in glowing terms of this marvelous new medium that girdles the earth, impressed by its speed. They told how wireless brought comfort and cheer to those in remote places, in the frozen north, on ships at sea; how the world's finest orchestras now visit our homes. Some even predicted the arrival of the millenium by the elimination of hatred and jealousy between nations, saying that "nation should speak peace unto nation." The failures of broadcasters as Murrow saw them---to accept their inherent responsibilities to seek truth wherever it might be found and to disseminate that truth as widely as possible---were only briefly and occasionally touched upon in comments by others in the field of broadcasting in the 1930s.

Murrow in his presentation also praised broadcasting's technical excellence. He noted, however, that though broadcasting had been subjected to some rather careful scrutiny, it had not yet been properly related to the social, political and economic structure that it inevitably reflects. As Murrow saw it, there had been too much blind acceptance of the broadcasters' statements of policy and principle. Twenty-one years later, at the twilight of his career, Murrow in a Chicago speech warned that commercialism had hindered the potentialities of television in a similar manner, and he then claimed that television as a great weapon for justice was "rusting in the scabbard."

For Murrow, content, not the medium, was paramount. "I would suggest," he once opined, "that the only way to judge broadcasting, national or international, is by what issues forth from your receiving set." The "message" emerges from the content, not the medium! This for Murrow was basic to understanding the role of the media.

What often issued forth, Murrow felt, were subtle and devious propaganda broadcasts, especially from such totalitarian states as Italy, Russia, Germany, and Spain. He worried about those Englishmen and Americans who could remain unconcerned about the power and influence of international broadcasting at the very time it was being used with considerable effectiveness to mold opinion by the fascist states, Nazi Germany in particular. For Murrow, it was not a question as to whether or not we should be in a race to achieve a dominant position in the highly effective field of propaganda. New and more powerful stations were being erected in order that nation could hurl invective at nation, so that news could be carefully selected and subjectively distorted in broadcasts to achieve national objectives. Whatever suspicion Murrow felt toward an unquestioning obedience to commercial broadcast policy, he also felt that the ever-increasing oppressive controls of government were not the answer.

Propaganda, its definitions and its uses, was very much on Murrow's mind that night. He believed---probably naively from the perspective of the contemporary world---that a responsible broadcasting organization should warn its listeners about propaganda. The problem, however, was that no broadcasting organization in the world of that day or in today's world could afford to warn listeners, because all use these devices. In that initial lecture, he noted that,

> there does not exist in my opinion such a thing as a broadcasting system without propaganda. We may make propaganda on behalf of the right to have monarchy or the status quo, or we may make propaganda on behalf of more tangible things such as cigarettes, soap or automobiles.

Although Murrow felt defensive about, perhaps even mildly ashamed of, "commercial" propaganda, he recognized a difference between that kind of mass persuasion for "selling soap," and the kind rich in potential for good or evil that deals with ideas rather than things.

When it came to selling things, Murrow noted, "Americans are without equal." Although the difference between propaganda on behalf of ideals and propaganda on behalf of products may be rather subtle, it is vital. People can suffer from smoking too much (and Edward R. Murrow was perhaps a particularly pertinent example of that) or buying too many cars, but such individual influences and choices that may or may not be influenced by broadcast propaganda could hardly be classed with the impact that could result from the mass acceptance of an immoral ideal or political objective.

In the lecture, Murrow described how arrangements had been made for broadcasts between England and the United States. In the preceding year, two networks had broadcast some 250 programs from Europe to America. They had varied from dart matches to opera, with art, culture, sports, and glimpses of daily life styles comprising the bulk of the programming. The age of international communication had indeed arrived, and Murrow was responsible for at least some of it.

Four decades later, one cannot help but reflect on the large number of broadcasts offered in that early period. Certainly these broadcasts in the late thirties were a drop in the proverbial bucket compared to the reports from around the world on today's major newscasts. On the other hand, aside from news events, how much attention is paid in the 1970s to the life and culture of diverse peoples living in other lands? Proportionately, very little indeed!

To Ed Murrow, in 1937, the purpose of these broadcasts was in no sense concerned with the improvement of Anglo- or Franco-American or any other European-relations with the United States. He believed in the "reflective mirror" theory of mass communication devoid of propaganda broadcasts, and he seemed intent on carrying it through. Murrow's theory might be summarized within that context as follows:

> We want to use this medium to hold an honest mirror to current conditions in England and in Europe. If there exists a vital difference of opinion, let us say on British foreign policy, we propose to reflect that difference of opinion.

Utilizing this approach, if something were reflected which might damage relations between the two countries, at least there could be no charge of propaganda if the speakers selected for the broadcasts were competent and so long as they reflected actual conditions and spoke the truth as they saw it. In short, Ed Murrow was intent on reporting "warts and all," as he was a quarter of a century later as Director of the United States Information Agency (USIA). For Murrow, the early period of development when radio was regarded as nothing more than an exciting toy or an electronic gimcrack was over.

From his first exposure to broadcast journalism, Murrow knew, partly intuitively, perhaps, and partly through his experience, that radio had to be *realistic*, in the full meaning of that term, to be effective. In the days of war ahead, his insistence on realism helped in large measure to establish this man as the broadcaster par excellence. In his speech that evening, he spelled out his broadcast philosophy quite casually, almost as an aside:

> It is difficult of course to make generalizations, but I should say that we have had more success with those people who talk less in terms of ideals, which leave most people cold, than in terms of things and people with which the listeners are familiar at first-hand.

Things and people, and specifics---these comprised the main foci of the emerging Murrow manner.

People in charge of communications media constituted a special interest for Murrow. Recognizing their tremendous power to shape and mold mass thinking, Murrow was concerned that most educators of that day remained "strangely indifferent concerning those who direct the affairs of broadcasting. They seldom ask, as they should, who makes these decisions, and what is his or her competence to do so."

Murrow wanted broadcasting to be first and foremost a medium of information and enlightenment. He knew that the nation, through its broadcasting system, might soon ask millions of people to risk their lives, and at that critical time broadcast journalism must be credible. If those who operated this medium failed to keep the citizenry informed of the problems and fundamental conflicts which determine national policy, then the first principle of democracy that requires an interested and aware electorate was being denied. Murrow recalled his work with radio in the 1936 political campaign, when he saw the power of this medium demonstrated at first-hand when utilized by Franklin Roosevelt. Even then, few people realized the potential power of radio in the political process.

Murrow, in his conclusion, acknowledged that, to date, radio had failed to fulfill its mission. And, for him, *mission* it had to be:

> There must be a greater definition of objective and an increasing sense of responsibility on the part of the broadcasters of the democracies. And above all we must

eliminate that unconscious major premise which causes us to believe that it is unwise or unsafe to provide our listeners with the information they desire . . .; the only alternative is to attempt to justify broadcasting because it entertains, but that is just like justifying newspapers because they carry funny pictures and cartoons.

Throughout his long career, Murrow never abandoned this view, nor did he ever concede that the major function of any mass medium was entertainment. He conceded that it was one function, perhaps, but it fell very low in his personal assessment of the uses of the medium. He reiterated this point many times. In 1959, for example, he noted publicly that television, like international radio at the dawn of World War II, if ill-used or neglected, was "merely lights and wires in a box." The medium, he emphasized, was not in itself the message:

It has enormous power, but it has no character, no conscience of its own. It reflects the hatreds, the jealousies and ambitions of those men and governments that control it. It can become a powerful force for mutual understanding between nations, but not until we have made it so.

In his Chatham House presentation, Murrow tried to make clear that his critique was not aimed at the BBC and its operations. The criticism in the speech could have been interpreted to apply to broadcasters in all English-speaking countries, or simply broadcasting wherever it existed. It could have been possible for a member of the BBC, listening to a young American talking about the failure of radio and calling for a higher purpose, to have been more than a little unimpressed, or even miffed. After all, though the nuances of approaches differed, Sir John Reith and British broadcasting for fifteen years had prided themselves on a noble vision of the use of broadcasting for the benefit of man. But, whether accepted or rejected, the lecture contained the basic philosophy that was to guide Edward R. Murrow in his communications efforts for the rest of his life. The British, like most Americans, would come to appreciate and applaud his approach in time. Meanwhile, it was quite obvious that the young CBS executive could learn a little more about the British and much more from the British. Indeed, for the next nine years, he did.

CHAPTER II

FIRST IMPRESSIONS: A SIZING UP

It was 1938 and another cold and dank spring fell on Europe bringing with it the ultimate challenge and final torment for another victim of German aggression, Austria. Bill Shirer couldn't get the media facilities to cover Hitler's takeover of his German neighbor, but a nearly empty chartered airplane arrived in Vienna by way of Warsaw and Berlin, and Ed Murrow was there. Amid static and random music, the British and American listeners heard a rather halting young voice crackling through the radio ether. One might upon hearing the broadcast muse that here was history being reported as it was actually occurring, a moment perhaps more significant in its full implications than the transmission of the letter "S" by Marconi. Murrow used radio in a way it never had been before, and every major crisis thereafter would find radio (and later television) reporters on the spot.

The people he had seen in Berlin had been calmly walking around as though no crisis of peace or war existed, and even Vienna seemed to be as he remembered it. But he described German storm troopers riding about the city, and each building had an armed German or Austrian Nazi guard. The word came directly from Vienna to the ears of a puzzled and interested America, puzzled as much by the reception of living, contemporary history as by the contents of the message itself.[1]

Darsie Gillie (then Miss Cecilia Reeves of the BBC) recalls Murrow's return to London following that historic broadcast:

> It was 2:30 in the morning when Murrow returned from Vienna at the time of the *Anschluss*. His text was shattering and when he had finished he asked me if I was very tired, because he had not slept since he came back and he would appreciate it if I would stay and have a drink and let him talk about it. I had many Austrian friends---all Jewish---and was hungry for news; we sat for about an hour while he told me the first of those stories of beating up in bars, and so on, with which we were to become all too familiar later.

By the end of that year, listeners in America would hear an Orson Welles' broadcast and would rush from their homes seeking shelter from Martian invaders, though one 12-year-old girl

---

[1]For a detailed account of this international news report by Edward R. Murrow, see Alexander Kendrick's *Prime Time*, Boston: Little Brown, 1969.

reported to the press that she "knew very well that the broadcast was just a story." Most of her elders, however, had become more nervous---and perhaps more ready to believe in catastrophe---as a result of the eyewitness broadcasts of crisis events in Europe. Some immediately thought of Hitler and suspected that the "Martian" invasion was another one of his tricks.

Before the year 1938 was over, Murrow chalked up a record number of broadcasts as he sought to inform millions of Americans about European affairs. He participated in some 35 transmissions, and he arranged or was indirectly concerned with a total of 151 shortwave programs from other points in Europe. He was a very busy man, this new CBS European Director. In addition to learning a new job, Murrow spent his time looking for help in building a staff, developing his own beat, arranging broadcasts of events, and working closely with people in and around his London base. He needed the cooperation of numerous people, and he apparently received it from many. What kind of impression did he make on those he met and with whom he interacted during this early period? The following vignettes convey some idea of his reception.

Sir Lindsay Wellington, former Director of Sound Broadcasting for the BBC and Controller of Programmes, remembers Murrow as "young, handsome, with piercing eyes, and a rather big head, not in the slang sense but in literal dimensions." Wellington recalls that he was dressed elegantly, but not very formally: "A good dresser, rarely a formal dresser."

Leonard Miall, later Controller of Overseas and Foreign Relations for the BBC, had some early memories of Murrow. Miall joined the BBC in 1939, but recalls a meeting three years earlier before Murrow had become the CBS European Director. It was during the summer, and Miall had gone to Sweden to attend a conference organized by the International Student Service. "Ed was a very earnest young man who was the secretary of this organization, and that was where I first got to know him. He was very much concerned with the problem of fascism and Naziism as it affected students and academics." Miall's first impression of "a very earnest, young Christian secretary of a do-gooding organization" was not uncommon. Others sensed this quality in Murrow at various times. It seemed to Miall always to be a striking part of the man's character.

This was the only time that Miall encountered Murrow until he dealt with him professionally after Vienna and during the war. He vividly remembered the Munich broadcasts:

> By this time the experience he [Murrow] had had in Vienna in 1938 had been developed a great deal. And there was, the whole time of Munich, this constant interruption of regular broadcasting by particularly Bill Shirer, Ed Murrow and [Hans Von] Kaltenborn. They were the people who seemed to interrupt programming all the time with flashes, as things seesawed through the Munich crisis. It wasn't any surprise to me that the famous Orson Welles Mars invasion

thing which occurred about a month after that had such a
grip on people, because of its verisimilitude.

The interruption of programs with news flashes, however, was a
fresh experience for millions of people at the time. The frequently ominous nature of the news flashes helped to attract
the attention of the listening public. In the United States,
this was particularly true following the Japanese attack on
Pearl Harbor.

Godfrey Talbot, a trained journalist who "joined the BBC
from a newspaper to get away from the news," had been BBC Public Relations Officer in the North Region until war broke out.
Then it was London, the news staff at Broadcast House, and a
job as one of the senior subeditors. This articulate, energetic
man later was given the assignment of royal reporter, covering
events pertaining to the British Sovereign. In searching his
memory, Talbot assessed Murrow as follows: "I had the clearest
impression of Ed, of this lean, saturnine, laconic, never-sleeping figure." So did others, Talbot felt:

Everybody thinks of him, of course, as this tall, dark,
lean figure. Someone had said he was an impressive,
majestic figure. I wouldn't use the word "impressive"
. . . "majestic," no . . . but he had an intensity even
before he opened his mouth that made you look twice.
You know, the sort of man who saw through a brick wall,
much further than most of us do. He was a piercing man,
piercing in the eye, in the inner calmness that looked
at something.

In 1933, the year that Hitler came to power in Germany,
Michael Balkwill joined the BBC as a junior subeditor to prepare the news for broadcasting. According to Balkwill, the
system worked something like this: "You are given by the
chief subeditor or duty editor the items in the news that he
wants covered with an indication of their length and a rough
outline of their treatment, and from the sources---you've got
the agency tape or your own reporters, or what---you prepare
a version which will be read by the announcer." Balkwill
worked in the BBC newsroom during the remainder of the thirties and throughout the war, so he saw a lot of Ed Murrow.
"He was an extremely good conversationalist," he said of
Murrow. "One felt immediately that he was most affable, most
charming, most formidably skillful at the job. It was a joy
to talk to him. Everybody felt this."

Author D. G. Bridson recalled coming down to the BBC to
run the documentary section when war broke out. He had been
a writer and producer in Manchester for some five years. He
kept running into Ed, and said that no one could possibly be
with Ed and watch him in the studio without being convinced
that he was a tremendously professional broadcaster, "that
he had a wonderfully incisive style, that he was a man of
independence and integrity, and a magnificent reporter. That

was the first thing that struck me and the first thing that struck anyone at the BBC who came across him."

When Bridson was prodded by the suggestion that his favorable impressions of Murrow's style were based on merely watching a person at the microphone, he responded with the sensitive writer's interpretation of detail:

> The way he played to the microphone, he was playing AT the microphone in a way that gave the listener as clear an impression of Ed's personality as the camera gave the television viewer.

CBS London correspondent Charles Collingwood relaxed into pleasant recollection when asked for his first impressions of his former boss. He smiled nostalgically and thought back on those early days.

Collingwood had been in London as a Rhodes scholar. When war broke out in 1939, he didn't want to return home. It seemed to him that the war would involve the United States eventually, but he felt he couldn't stay on at Oxford when his generation of Englishmen were all going to war. "I came very close to joining the British Army," he said. Instead, he got a job with the United Press, and worked for nearly two years in England and Amsterdam. Collingwood worked nights, and one of his jobs was to cover the blitz. He recalls standing on top of the office roof with his tin helmet and a map of the city. He would spot where the big fires were, send someone to cover them, or would cover them himself. He finally joined CBS in the early months of 1941.

Did he recall his first meeting with Ed Murrow? "Yes, of course I do," he chuckled:

> It was strange. Ed already had become a household word in the United States, but we'd never met, and I didn't know who he was. I came into my office and there was a note on my desk to call what I thought was a Mr. Morrell at CBS. So I called and asked for Mr. Morrell, and Kay Campbell, his secretary and associate, said "You mean Mr. Murrow." And I said, "Yes, I suppose I do."

Collingwood explained that Murrow had been looking for someone to work in radio, in the London bureau. He wanted someone with reporting experience, but who had not, "to use his words, been contaminated by print." He felt that radio was a new medium, and he didn't want people to come in with all the cliches of print journalism. Collingwood wasn't certain whether Murrow had exaggerated this distinction, but he knew that Murrow felt strongly about radio as a new and novel medium. Someone had told him that there was "a young American working at the United Press . . . me." Collingwood continued:

> He set up a lunch at the Savoy, which at the time was sort of the headquarters for American journalists. I mean, it was the place where everyone went, and had a

very good lunch, and he said he was almost put off
because I was wearing a very loud pair of argyle
socks, plaid---you know, bright colors. Ed was
always very conservative in his dress, and he wasn't
quite sure what this meant about my character; but
in any event, a few weeks later I did a test for him
for New York.

Another tall, distinguished, silver-haired colleague---Eric Sevareid---remembers the first time he spent an evening at the home of the Murrows, an evening that provided him with his first experience watching television. "I was a kid from Minneapolis," Sevareid recalled. It was in the fall of 1937, and he and his wife were invited over to the Murrow flat not far from the BBC. Sevareid had a letter of introduction from Jay Allen of the Chicago *Daily News*. The most memorable part of the evening was observing the play, *Journey's End*, on the small six-inch screen in the very large cabinet. Sevareid found that the sound and picture were quite good. He was astonished by the novelty of the new medium but dimly aware of its great future potential. Then the war came, British television ended, and Sevareid went to Paris to work for the Paris *Herald*.

Commenting on his impressions of Ed Murrow, Sevareid noted:

When you first met him, he made the most vivid impression on everybody. He was an extraordinarily attractive man, with that voice, those remarkable eyes. Great warmth and charm. Unforgettable fellow.

Writing at an earlier time, Sevareid had recalled the climate of opinion in pre-war Britain, much as a young John Kennedy had in his book, *Why England Slept*. Sevareid noted that most of the English were largely unconcerned about the Continent just before the war. Their leaders, though not the political ones, knew that their fellow countrymen were both unconcerned and ignorant. For Sevareid, it was obvious that

In this segment of leadership the British had something better than we had in our counterpart. The sheer brilliance, the articulate, unanswerable logic of the editorials and essays in the liberal journals took one's breath away. They were saying it better, more acutely than we---but to no more effect.

Sevareid was impressed by some of these men he met in Whitehall and Fleet Street. Though gracious enough in encounter, they wasted no time in small talk. But he was more impressed by a young American, "a tall, thin man with a boyish grin, extraordinary dark eyes that were alight and intense one moment and somber and lost the next." Sevareid felt that he seemed to possess that rare thing,

an instinctive, intuitive recognition of truth. . . .
His name was Edward R. Murrow. He talked about England
through half the night, and, although he had been there
only about a year, one went away with the impulse to
write down what he had said, to recapture his phrases,
so that one could recall them and think about them
later. I knew I wanted to listen to this man again,
and I had a strong feeling that many others ought to
know him.

Former *London Times* reporter Tom Barman remembers his first infrequent meetings with Murrow before and during the war. Barman's beat covered the low countries, Scandinavia and France until war broke out and he joined the Enemy Propaganda Department of the Government. Later, he served for twenty years as a diplomatic correspondent with the BBC. When queried about Murrow, he replied:

My impression was that he was a tremendous chap with
enormous vitality, with enormous resources inside him
which would come out particularly in his broadcasts.
At parties you would see Murrow and you felt he was
more an ordinary chap, but you felt a great reserve
of strength there. He had the quality which you
associate with a virile movie actor.

The word was not much in use then, but today we would call this quality "charisma." It was a kind of charisma that apparently was observed and felt by most people, whether they had just met him or their knowledge of him came from longer association. Ed Murrow, very young indeed, physically attractive, strong, personable: this was the man whose power of utterance would tell America of Britain's plight, who would organize and direct the staff that, along with his own reporting, would transform world communications. These were first impressions at the beginning of an innovative and tempestuous career.

CHAPTER III

ON THE JOB: WAR COMES TO AN ADJUSTING BBC

When Hitler sent his Panzer divisions smashing into Poland, a new world of communications began to evolve. Ed Murrow would not only be a part of it; he would, to some considerable extent, lead it. The Nebraska farm wife, the New Yorker, the resident of the emerging suburb would never be the same. No more would news come to the house only in the form of cold, dark marks on a page. Nor would it come after the passage of some time. It would come through the air, at once, in the hot immediacy of radio. It would come by voice. Among the most prominent voices was that of Ed Murrow.

Hitler at first stalked his victims, slyly warding off his main enemies---Britain, France, and the Soviet Union---as the morsels of Austria and Czechoslovakia were bitten off and gulped. At last there was Poland, and war. The democracies finally mobilized their collective will to resist as well as their military forces. Decisions were made. Confusion over how to deal with Adolf Hitler was gone. There was only the heady awareness of unity. Perhaps the world's last confrontation between good and evil, in the classic sense, was about to begin. The agony of hope that it would not be necessary to fight a major war was over. Now, in the immortal words of Winston Churchill, it would be only "blood, tears, toil and sweat." How long the agony would last no one knew.

This story would reach the ears of Murrow's countrymen through his reports. His task: to describe the cataclysmic encounter between democracy and fascism. The man who had helped German scientists find jobs and security in the States during the thirties, who had visited Vienna, had no doubt about which side had to win the ultimate victory. His role was to tell the unfolding story. That meant words, paper, travel, danger, a little car buzzing about London, bombs, talk, thinking, interpreting, moderating, listening, interviewing.

Michael Standing, former BBC administrator for radio, had been controller of the entertainment side of radio programming and, before that, had headed the "outside" broadcasts division. In 1939, the times were, in his words, traumatic for the BBC and the country after the frenetic build-up for war. Observers had anticipated a sudden massive Nazi air attack on the country, and an immediate total war in Continental Europe. Neither happened. The BBC was left in a state of suspended animation, as all was silent, day after day, week after week. Known as the "phony war," it was phony, indeed.

The BBC provided numerous background programs that together reflected a mood of expectancy that was not fulfilled. In the lull that ensued, it was necessary to come back to reality, and this was a painful process. Professor Asa Briggs of the University of Sussex, in his monumental third volume chronicling the history of the BBC, detailed the problem to which Standing had referred:

> The passion for "news" was insatiable during the first days of the war in Poland, but there was confusion in the newly-founded Ministry of Information, suspicion in Press circles, of the BBC entering into serious competition with the newspapers "to their detriment" and an inadequate sense within the BBC itself of the key importance of news as a major wartime service.[1]

Just as it did in America, the press-radio war droned on in England. The BBC had agreed during those prewar years that it would not broadcast news prior to 6:00 p.m. or later than 2:00 a.m. There was no regular BBC foreign news service and no staff of foreign news correspondents. There was, however, reorganization when war came. New programs and new plans, and many programs of recorded music were incorporated into the BBC format. Memos were circulated, and conferences were held. An expectant audience heard little about the war upon which it was supposed to be embarked.

The great geared-up machine had no place to go, and so it faltered and sputtered. Still, new techniques and methods had to be developed. News reporting via radio was not yet up to the challenge of war. Referring to eyewitness accounts and actual sounds of war, Briggs says that "no attention was paid . . . to the first halting steps taken to include direct news reporting in the BBC programmes." And this was nearly two months after war had been declared.

In point of fact, the world's oldest national broadcasting service simply was not ready for this reportorial task. For all his powerful leadership, perhaps the late Sir John Reith, the BBC's early guiding Director General, had placed---symbolically and actually---too much of the cloak of the dinner jacket around the BBC announcer. It may have been a kind of condescension toward an outside world that prohibited the airing of such commonplace sounds as the voice of a firsthand witness to a spectacular event. After all, from the stodgy, early BBC perspective, that witness might be just a *plain citizen*. And the rude sound of a bomb or bullet might open the BBC to criticism that it was overdramatizing events.

In short, the BBC philosophy and activity were not "ready made" for a bright American observer to pick up and apply. The BBC had to learn, as did the untrained Mr. Murrow. They would learn and grow together. Perhaps each influenced and affected the other, but that is running ahead of the story.

One event illustrates how this process of learning and growing together occurred. It was a Saturday afternoon, the second

---

[1] Briggs, Asa, *The War of Words*, Vol. III (London: Oxford University Press, 1970), p. 80. Many important viewpoints and conclusions on BBC operations found in this chapter are a reflection of Briggs' definitive volume.

day of September, 1939. Cecilia Reeves, who had been sworn in that morning as a censor, but had not yet read the rules, was on duty at the BBC. She was asked to clear a line to CBS in New York for Ed Murrow. She had been instructed that lines could only be connected if a qualified censor of military material were present. She recalled that Ed "always ad-libbed; I was non-plussed but aware of the excitement it would cause in America if they were told Ed's broadcast would not take place for reasons of censorship, so I rushed off to find the D.G. [Director General]." She said that he thought she was worried about the problem of placating Ed's feelings. "As I was explaining that my reasons for concern were quite different, I suddenly realized that Ed had a script, as he was going to read [Polish statesman, Ignace] Paderewski's declaration [to the Polish nation]." She returned to the studio, knowing that there was no military information in the Polish statesman's declaration, and proclaimed that a censor had seen the script, and the broadcast was transmitted.

As the day progressed, the situation grew increasingly tense. Reeves ended up again on night duty, working for the Scrutineer's Unit which was charged with censorship of military information. Poland was already at war. The big question had not yet been answered: What would Britain do? After Munich, after one evasion after another, what would His Majesty's Government decide? At the peak period for the evening spot, about 2:00 a.m. (9:00 p.m. in New York), the American correspondents came to the microphone one after another, each giving the same message---reasonably deduced, one could suppose, from past experience---that, once again, England would back down.

As the American correspondents proceeded to deliver that message in the form of a prediction, there was one notable exception. One man, after nearly three years on this tiny island, had read the British character differently. Ed Murrow filed his analysis last with Cecilia Reeves. She recalled that he handed her his text and asked, "Am I right on this? I've got to be right!" Years later she noted that he had a happy knack of summing up a situation with a quotation, often one from Shakespeare. On this eve of war, he paraphrased the quotation from a similar occasion in Macbeth. His text began, "Stands England where she did? I think she does."

Here, then, are the actual words reported by Edward R. Murrow in that historic script of September 2, 1939:

> Some people have told me tonight that they believe a big deal is being cooked up which will make Munich and the betrayal of Czechoslovakia look like a pleasant tea party. I find it difficult to accept this thesis. I don't know what's in the mind of the government, but I do know that to Britishers their pledged word is important. . . . Most observers here agree that this country is not in the mood to accept a temporary solution. And that's why *I believe that Britain in the end of the day will stand where she is pledged to stand*, by the side of Poland in a war that is now in progress.

Reeve's experience that evening reminded her of an earlier event when Ed Murrow had also distinguished himself in her eyes:

> About Munich, I remember only that he shared the general shame and misery; and in particular, he seemed to be the only correspondent who had taken the trouble to phone Jan Masaryk, who had been sitting all day waiting for someone from the Foreign Office to tell him what was happening; and no one had.

The basic structure of British broadcasting had been established prior to the outbreak of war, and the potentialities for effective coverage of war events were there. Briggs has noted that, "The BBC had many assets in September, 1939---a group of people, particularly in engineering and production; a structure which allowed for considerable flexibility; a tested policy of telling the truth and 'nothing but the truth, even if the truth is horrible.'" The latter part of that statement was borrowed by Briggs from a vigorous Scotsman who headed the Home Service desk, R. T. Clark. "Telling the truth," maintained Clark, "is the only way to strengthen the morale of the people whose morale is worth strenghtening." Churchill's many blunt, factual statements concerning military reverses during the early period of the war were obviously based on a similar philosophy. Murrow spent many hours in R. T. Clark's office throughout the war, and, directly or indirectly, this philosophy nurtured and reinforced Murrow's own temperament.

Still, the lumbering BBC had its problems in the early months of 1940. As already noted, one difficulty grew out of the fact that there was really little in the way of a war to report; government and broadcasting objectives were mutually confused and confusing. Finally the Ministry of Information called a meeting in April of 1940 which was attended by the members of the highest echelon of the BBC. Concerning that meeting, Briggs reported:

> All the misunderstandings came out into the open, with the BBC being forced into the defensive from the start. The BBC was singled out for its own handling of news, most of which had been handed out to it. . . . It was clear that the BBC was being made the scapegoat for the failure of the government to lead and to plan.

The top brass of the BBC also raised the problem that there was a general reluctance on the part of the armed services to provide more broadcasts by naval, military, and air experts probably for security reasons. Moreover, news often was simply withheld until after the Germans had broadcast it, or so at least argued the BBC staffers. To cite an example, they noted that there had been no prompt British report on the German raid on Scapa Flow on March 16, 1940. The Germans were first to broadcast their version of what happened before the British even admitted that there had been an engagement. Ed Murrow knew the significance of telling the British viewpoint of events, and he, among other correspondents, complained publicly in a broadcast one week after the raid. "My own attempt," he said, "to see what the Germans did at Scapa Flow has also met with failure. So far as I know, no correspondent, neutral or otherwise, has visited Scapa since the raid."

The Germans actually broadcast news of the Scapa Flow raid to the United States eight or nine hours before the BBC. When Prime Minister Neville Chamberlain admitted in the House of Commons on March 19, 1940, that the raid had been a "failure," the German radio retorted the same day with the statement that "the rest of the world has no more faith in the official British War Communiques." Defending the BBC's policies and practices, Briggs concedes that there was a general and widespread skepticism about the truth of ALL war news; yet he refers to a *Fortune* survey of December, 1939, which showed that, as of that date, British news commanded more public confidence in the United States than did German or Italian news, and slightly more than French news. Such attitudes might have been directly attributable to America's closer historical and cultural affinity to Britain, rather than to any policy of BBC reporting.

Early in 1940, the BBC's lines of communication branched out in several directions at home and abroad, and interpretations of reports from abroad were also made available to the home audience. People listened not only to what was projected deliberately at them, but also to what was projected at somebody else, and above all to what was projected for home consumption. This procedure was necessary if people, particularly journalists, were to evaluate properly the status of thinking in Britain. If an American journalist wanted to get at the temper of Great Britain, he would pay little attention to what was being said to America but very precise attention to what was being broadcast from Britain to Europe and to people at home.

In terms of basic policy objectives, then, the BBC staff determined in the early part of the war that it was imperative that consistency and objectivity dominate both domestic and foreign broadcasting. Some British critics demanded that BBC policy utilize the dramatic effect of German propaganda---to fight fire with fire, so to speak. The official line, however, remained that of telling the same truth to everyone and to address even "individual Germans" as an Englishman or Frenchman would speak to them if they could meet in a neutral cafe. While there was to be no ranting and raving (a decidedly un-British manner of doing things, anyway), there was "ample scope for 'virility, vigour, and emotion.'" Gradually, in spite of errors and delays, BBC officials believed that such a policy would in time build up a European audience that could count on the BBC for its candid presentation of the same basic news to all countries. This, then, was the approach to the problems of matching policy to programs at the beginning of the war as described by the BBC's main chronicler, Asa Briggs.

When the European roof fell in with the end of the "Sitzkrieg" and the beginning of the "Blitzkrieg" in the spring of

1940, there was little time for reflection about these policies. The immediate demand was for the BBC to try to keep up with events that were unfolding with unprecedented speed. Ways of informing a concerned populace without too great a risk that such information would give aid and comfort the enemy had yet to be found. Rumors spread throughout Britain during the Norwegian campaign simply because the Admiralty, headed still by Winston Churchill, released too little official news, and the government was embarrassed by Churchill's early optimistic public statements which were not warranted by events.

From the evidence that Professor Briggs presents, it is reasonable to conclude that, before the Blitzkrieg, BBC news reporting was indeed slower than that of the Germans. The BBC discouraged or, at the very least, deemphasized the use of on-the-spot reports. There was also a lack of support for an approach that emphasized the interpretation of events, and there was a general need for clarifying the approach to the use of radio for war reportage. Was it a need to make a gradual shift from its time-tested philosophy, as the result of technical innovations, or was it the fact that events produced an entirely new age and an entirely new set of demands which in turn produced a need for fundamental adjustments? No one can say for certain which was the cause and which the effect.

When France fell, England's attitude toward that divided country was ambivalent, and the problems noted above became ever more pressing and complex. The official attitude toward Marshall Henri Philippe Petain, the new French leader who negotiated surrender, was a cautious one. This posed the question within the BBC of how should such a policy be handled? It is a comment on the respect with which Ed Murrow was held that Cecilia Reeves asked for his advice on how best to handle the situation. Murrow took the long view, thinking ahead to the continuing important relations between Britain and France. Her dilemma, however, came up against harsh reality when she broadcast a report attacking Petain. "It seemed," she said, "that half the French in London attacked me for attacking Petain; the other half for paying him any mind, or not attacking him enough." When Reeves first requested his advice, Murrow was reluctant to comment. "I don't know anything about France," he replied. "Never mind that," she responded. "As a human being, what do you think?" His reply: "Petain is necessary now for France. Attack his policy. To attack him personally would be disastrous." Briggs also notes this incident in which the American reporter assisted in the formation of a sensitive and important policy of the BBC. By that time it was obvious that Ed Murrow had achieved the respect and even the admiration of many British and those in the BBC in particular.

Bickering and struggling over formulation of policy and its application came to an end in the fall of 1940. By then, London was burning. As German bombs rained down, the feeling within the BBC was that the German propaganda machine was not measurably superior to the British. As reports on the raids came in from both the BBC and from the Germans, belief in BBC news reporting was restored, for it soon became evident that the Germans engaged in gross exaggeration. An added factor, of course, must have been that the bombing of London and other British cities unified a people so cohesively that belief in whatever German news sources reported had descended to zero. Admittedly, however, British accuracy during such a crisis was not absolute. They, too, exaggerated. Says Briggs: "The Air Ministry never implied that the figures released each day were provisional, and the statistics had an important psychological effect on a country fighting for its life." Both sides, therefore, exaggerated the other's loss of planes, with the Germans, however, exaggerating a bit more.

Referring to a report on a German propaganda attack on Britain released in late November of 1940, Briggs remarked how curious it was that so much importance was attached to the British party system as a foil for German propaganda. The report indicated that the enemy's propaganda technique would probably fail against any country with a vigorous, healthy party system for three reasons: (1) the range of plausible misrepresentation was not unlike that with which a party member was familiar, (2) the party system would provide protection against plain lying, and (3) a party system depends on the existence of a network of ideas and institutions in which the relationship between ideas and actions is continuously discussed and tested.

Briggs also suggested that someone else had a simpler explanation for the ineffectiveness of German propaganda:

> Perhaps Ed Murrow got nearer to the truth. Recognizing that there was room for many opinions about the diplomatic, economic and military policy of the British government, he noted quietly before the great air blitz on London began that ordinary Londoners were made of stern stuff. "They can take what is coming."

Gradually the BBC came to improve its news services and reporting. At the time, the techniques seemed perhaps more revolutionary than evolutionary; by today's sophisticated approaches, the improvements seem rather obvious and rudimentary. Nevertheless, they established the base from which later news broadcast organizations and individuals would expand and grow. Among the developments were: gathering news reports from on-the-spot war reporters, expanding outside contacts, using recorded sounds and inserts in news programs, experimenting with special news programs, associating comment with fact, and, above all, as Briggs summarized it, "gaining an enhanced sense of professionalism."

This, then, was the milieu in which Edward R. Murrow worked during the early war years. As the BBC developed and grew, he was there to grow with it, to learn from it, and, certainly, to contribute to its better functioning.

CHAPTER IV

ED MURROW AS BROADCASTER, MODERATOR, AND ADMINISTRATOR:

AN EVALUATION BY HIS WARTIME COLLEAGUES

    A reporter has a job to do, and so does an administrator. What was Ed Murrow's main responsibility as he began to function as the first "radio journalist"? His predecessor, Cesar Searchinger, had functioned simply as an administrator who arranged talks. With the war's onset and spread, Ed Murrow's job became much more than that of administrator.
    In a general sense, his role was to keep the American public informed of developments in Britain, and to arrange to have direct news reports made from other European locations. In short, his responsibility was to do whatever necessary to report this greatest of all wars from direct, on-the-spot locations whenever possible.
    Murrow's home was all of London, but specifically Studio B-4 in the basement of that odd-looking structure, Broadcast House, located on Portland Place near Oxford Circus in central London. His Hallam Street flat was nearby, easy walking distance away.
    Murrow took part in a panel discussion program called "Freedom Forum" throughout the war, sometimes as a panelist, other times as moderator of the show. Early in the war he appeared on a program called "Meet Uncle Sam," and occasionally he broadcast a "Sunday Postscript" to the news. There were also a few specialty programs. In one, "People in the News," Murrow broadcast a portrait of General Dwight D. Eisenhower. In another, entitled "And So to Bed," he read from one of his favorite authors, James Thurber. On still another program, he talked about *Uncle Tom's Cabin* as an example of "Books that Made History." Rarely, but on a few occasions, he wrote a piece for one of the London papers. Thus he communicated to some limited extent with the British while he devoted most of his efforts to communicating with the American people.
    In an interview in the *News Chronicle* in 1941, Murrow described the handling of his broadcasts:

> Twice each day a transatlantic telephone circuit is opened between London and New York. . . . When the conversation is finished, both of us watching the second hand on the clock, he [the engineer] says "Cue coming up," a switch is thrown in New York, and I hear an announcer over there saying, "Go ahead, London."[1]

---

[1] *News Chronicle* (London), February 26, 1941.

Stressing that this routine had been established before the war, Murrow added, "That means that for the next five, ten, or fifteen minutes, whatever is said from London goes out over 125 transmitters scattered all over the United States."

Murrow himself felt that this daily procedure was of supreme importance, noting that "This is the first planned, consistent effort in American broadcasting to deliver to its listeners an adult news service, which is heard in America one twenty-third of a second after it is spoken in London." The Idaho sheep rancher, the California fruit grower, the steelworker in Pittsburgh, and millions of others could hear Ed's broadcasts through their loudspeakers by merely tuning to their local radio stations. Within a quarter-hour, men from London, Berlin, and Rome would report news and, as far as Ed Murrow was able to influence the operation, would make every effort to be temperate, responsible, and mature in selecting the manner in which they made the facts of war known to their fellow countrymen at home. Many of the news items produced in this manner could not be found in official communiques and announcements.

How did each night's broadcast actually get underway? Writing in an issue of *Time and Tide*, Murrow put it this way: "Every night about midnight I go down to the basement of the BBC and do a broadcast to the U.S. of A. Before the broadcast begins there is always five or ten minutes conversation between the engineers in London and New York."[2] The purpose of the talk was to test the quality of the transatlantic shortwave telephone circuit. The conversations might be about the current price of Brussels sprouts or holidays, but certainly never about the war.

"Often," Murrow noted, we can hear Cairo, Ankara, Berlin or Moscow also testing circuits to New York. From four or five points in Europe voices are going out across the Atlantic, preparing a fifteen-minute broadcast which may include originations from four warring capitals." One night Murrow mentioned that in testing the circuit the line was excellent from Cairo, but when he asked how the London to New York circuit was, word came back, "Not bad, but it seems to have suffered a slight degradation in the last few minutes." Murrow, always ready with a quick retort, responded, "I hope you meant the technical quality of the circuit."

On one occasion, Ed Murrow joined with his NBC competitor, Fred Bate, to discuss their work over the air to the British. F. H. Grisewood, host of the "World Goes By" series, had invited them to come and discuss their jobs on the program in which Grisewood brought to the microphone "people in the news, people talking about the news, and interesting visitors to Britain."

Fred Bate asked Ed to begin, noting that each probably would say about the same thing. He began with basics. "The first thing you need for a broadcast to the States is a microphone and a studio." Then the all-important circuit which, he noted, was made

---

[2]*Time and Tide* (London), July 19, 1941. Murrow's views as guest writer appeared in a column entitled "Notes on the Way."

available to them any time they wanted it, twenty-four hours a day.

When it came time for the actual broadcast to begin, he noted that "The BBC and the [British] Post Office provide the engineers to turn the knobs and twist the dials and do all sorts of strange things that neither one of us understands." Fred Bate then discussed the American "network" and what it meant, time differentials, and other technical problems. Then Murrow noted one inescapable fact about broadcast journalism: "If we say the wrong word, it's gone---you can't bring it back and erase it." That's still a problem with some on-the-spot reports, even in an age of video tape.

During the discussion, Fred Bate asked Murrow if he now calculated in Greenwich Mean Time, if it had in fact become second nature with him. "No, it never will," he replied. "When a rush cable comes in from New York asking for a special broadcast at five in the morning, I never can remember whether I should say 'Good morning,' or 'Good evening' because it's only midnight in New York."

During the discussion, Murrow revealed the favorite part of his beat. "I like the House of Commons best. I like to sit in that rather dingy little room, listen to speeches and debates, then jump in a cab, go up to the studio, and try to take Americans right through the window and into the [Commons'] room." The Commons meant the British parliamentary system and democracy to Murrow, and later, when he was to leave Britain, his tribute to the nation was his observation that even in the heat of war the parliamentary system with its recognition of the value of the role of the Opposition had survived. Murrow also loved an argument, and he could get his fill of that in the Commons. "Sometimes," Murrow felt, "it's possible to give listeners in America something of the feel of the House, not only what is said, but who was there and what they looked like . . . a little glimpse of history being made."

The program ended with Fred Bate's observation: "Has it struck you that we've been talking about ourselves to people some of whom we might see any minute? There's no 3,000 miles of water between us this time, Ed." Murrow responded, "That's a frightening thought, isn't it?"

Perhaps there was a comforting security in the separation of the two countries. It made the job of reporting to America a different and probably easier task than that of communicating on the BBC to the British. Americans had no direct impressions of the war, but only those molded and shaped by the news media and the broadcast journalists.

In addition to appearing as a guest on BBC programs, Murrow often moderated the "Freedom Forum" programs and appeared as a guest in more than 150 such programs throughout the war. In addition to Murrow, regulars in the series were Sir Frederick Whyte, George Malcolm Young, and Murrow's good friend, Harold Laski. A variety of topics were discussed, some dealing with the war situation and many with questions about the postwar period.

As moderator, Murrow listened well in these programs, speaking seldom but attempting to draw out those who had little to say, and he tried to get the group to reach a consensus, at least on some aspect of the question. Often he would introduce the topic, give whatever definitions were needed, and perhaps the American viewpoint as he saw it. In his role as moderator, Ed Murrow was already getting excellent training for his later role as a television interviewer for "Person to Person" and the "See It Now" series.

In addition to being a broadcaster, Murrow was busily engaged as an administrator, working in two directions. He had to hire staff, plan their activities, and deal with BBC officials in making arrangements. Eric Sevareid, in his book *Not So Wild a Dream*,[3] has recalled how he was hired by Ed Murrow. At the time, he was working at the Paris *Herald* by day and the United Press at night. The president of United Press, Hugh Baillie, had arrived from New York and offered him an excellent new position. Sevareid sat alone in his office, trying to think it out. It would be an excellent opportunity to write on the coming war, but could he function within an agency system where the measurement of success was which story had received "top billing" in the headlines rather than writing quality or factual accuracy? Then the phone rang. It was Murrow. He told Sevareid he didn't know much about his experience, but liked the way he wrote and liked his ideas. "There's only Shirer and Grandin and myself now," Murrow commented, "but I think this thing may develop into something." Murrow assured Sevareid that there would be no pressure to provide scoops or anything sensational. Just the honest news, and if there wasn't any, why, just say so.

Sevareid recalled his audition with some degree of horror. He thought it would be on closed circuit for a few New York executives, but two hours before the broadcast he learned that his talk would be heard over the entire CBS network. The result: "Hastily I wrote a new speech on contemporary affairs and delivered it before the microphone with my hands shaking so violently that listeners must have heard the paper rattling."

New York liked the material, but not his presentation. "That's all right, I'll fix it," Murrow told Sevareid. Murrow advised him to quit his jobs anyway. He did so, against the advice of friends, but as Sevareid put it, there was something about Ed Murrow that evoked a feeling of trust. A distinguished reporting career followed for Sevareid, first in France until that fateful June of 1940 when the French capitulated. He then made his way to England via merchant ship, where British immigration officials were more than mildly suspicious of his explanations. Murrow again "fixed things," all the way from the Home Office in London to the immigration inspector.

---

[3]Sevareid, Eric, *Not So Wild a Dream* (New York: Alfred A. Knopf, 1946), pp. 106-8.

In his relations with the BBC's American Liaison Unit, Richard Marriott recalls that, while Ed was forceful and competitive in trying to get the news, he was an easy man to deal with. BBC files, however, reveal that Murrow could be both tactful and reproachful in his dealings with BBC officials. Roger Eckersley, who directed the American unit for a time, wrote to Murrow asking him to confirm his belief that American broadcasting correspondents were not offered facilities for visits to places equal to those offered the press. Eckersley indicated that print journalists were able to visit certain factories and docks to which the broadcasters were not invited. Murrow replied that, in general, the impression he had was that facilities offered to broadcasters were equal to those proffered to American print reporters, although there might be some slip-ups on occasion. "As you know," he commented, "newspapermen complain constantly that we broadcasters get all the breaks. So the odds are probably about even." Certainly this was a tactful reply to such a letter.

On another occasion, however, Murrow had prodded Eckersley to get a member of his staff on a planned night patrol of the Thames. Eckersley replied that he needed more information and said he was reluctant to ask the Admiralty for facilities since their public relations officer had arranged the trip. Murrow's answer was blunt: "I detect a certain note of mild reproach. . . . I have not the least sympathy for the overworked Public Relations Officer at the Admiralty, particularly since I have just finished about six weeks of night work for the Admiralty." This comment referred to a commentary he had done for a film which would go to the States. He added that he was prepared to send Charles Collingwood out on the night patrol on the Thames any time it could be arranged. Tact, concession, irritation, prodding---all were combined in the process of administering an office so that his reporters could cover many areas and events.

What potential news source remained untapped for the broadcast journalists? How about Iceland? "There is no urgency about it," he wrote Eckersley, "but I do think that a couple of talks from the one area successfully invaded by Britain would have a salubrious effect on our audience." In one memorandum in late summer of 1940 he suggested, in addition to the Iceland trip, a visit to Gibraltar, a ride on a coastal vessel, a trip on a torpedo boat, and a night at an observation post on the coast. He also wanted a reporter to fly with the coastal command patrol, perhaps between Scotland and Norway, a visit to an internment camp to describe the living conditions, a visit to the London docks to describe arrival of ships with provisions, a night flight over London, and a report from Cairo. And, finally, "I should like to send someone to observe a busy day at the Bow Street Police Court, when the Court is dealing with minor offenses, in order to produce a broadcast on the general lines of British justice in action during wartime." Quite a listing, indeed, but together they tend to give some small indication of the imaginative reportorial mind and style of Edward R. Murrow at this stage of his career.

Thus Murrow's job consisted of clearing permissions through the BBC for specific assignments, suggesting programs to be broadcast, employing and dispersing staff, settling issues with other broadcasters and his print competitors, overseeing relations with the other network (NBC), appearing on and involving himself with broadcasts for the BBC, and one other small chore: to report home himself on a daily basis. It was a busy time for the broadcaster-administrator.

In his capacities as administrator and as panelist on BBC programs, Ed Murrow served an obviously important function. He was the executive in London, the public relations officer of the Columbia Broadcasting System. Yet it was in his capacity as reporter that he became best known and made his greatest contribution during the war years. It is to that function that we must now turn our attention, and to those who were in a position to judge Murrow in an operating capacity.

One such person was Richard Marriott, who vividly remembers the unusual ability that Murrow had in obtaining information. Certainly the first function of the reporter is to learn before he can communicate. On Murrow's ability seemingly to always have necessary information stored up for use at appropriate times, Marriott noted the following:

> Ed had a strange capacity for acquiring information without seeming to do so. I always remember that when in his flat, you'd always see on his table two or three of the newest books about current affairs, politics, whatever. I never knew where he had time . . . I'd never caught Ed reading at any stage of my life. He somehow knew what was in them. It was as if he could kind of absorb a book.

Marriott speculated that either he read much more than anyone realized or simply skimmed, taking the essentials out of books. According to Marriott, Ed "always knew what were the latest books, and what they were about. He was tremendously good at being well-informed about whatever was happening."

The telephone was an instrument of great importance to Murrow in carrying out his work. Marriott says:

> He was a tremendous telephoner. Ed was always on the telephone to New York. We were . . . not a great telephoning country. Or weren't then. A transatlantic call was something you prepared for to get the most said in a minimum of time. But Ed would reach for the telephone rather like you'd reach for a cigarette. . . . I think he had a telephone beside his bath. . . . He wanted to be so accessible.

A reporter, before he can transmit the story, must of course have something to communicate. He gathers data; he ruminates; he experiences; he abstracts and generalizes from his data. Certainly in Ed Murrow's case, more than just the telephone was required for contacts. He had to meet with people, talk with them, go to the scene of the story, try to relive or reconstruct an event.

Sir Lindsay Wellington, for example, has noted that Murrow was extremely sociable when he was around Broadcast House, and that his sociability had a purpose other than relaxation. According to Sir Lindsay, Ed was always in search of information, news, opinions, and all these meetings were sharpening meetings for him. Cecilia Reeves (Mrs. Darsie Gillie) has corroborated this view, recalling one occasion, at a cocktail party for Ambassador Winant, when the two of them talked for half an hour about Admiral Jean Louis Darlan and his role in the Petain (Vichy) government. He wanted to know why people felt as they did about Darlan. He questioned constantly and did his homework, Reeves emphasized. Rather than hitting a story head-on in a regular sense, she noted, he would go around back to see what was there. Murrow often questioned reporters about how they got a story. Robert Reid, the Yorkshire newspaperman who joined the BBC before the war and later became an editor, recalls flying back after the liberation of Paris where he had broadcast the arrival of General Charles de Gaulle. In fact, Murrow's inquiry concerning that reporting job occurred months after the broadcast. According to Reid, "Ed wanted to know every single detail of where I was, what kind of microphone, how quickly had it taken to link up with the engineer, and how it was flown back to London."

Sir Lindsay Wellington often observed Murrow preparing a story through a great deal of verbalizing with associates: "When Ed was working up towards a piece, he could be talking a lot, in many words; I wouldn't say mumbling, he never mumbled at all, but he could be going to and fro before he found his way." He would talk around a subject, and while ruminating over a pipe or many cigarettes in front of a fire, he would be discursive as he was getting ready to think about "subject A." Sir Lindsay noted that there were two parts to the process of getting the story down on paper: (1) mapping out what he was going to say; and (2) punching it home, saying the piece in his own way. He elaborated further on these points:

> By the time he [Murrow] had finished that thinking and by the time he got himself down to the process of writing, he'd got it all squeezed up tight. . . . You're first ruminating around the subject; you're gradually coming to the heart of it. You're needing to stop and research just to pick up certain key facts. Then it begins to jell. At this point you take hold of it and squeeze it tight, and put it in your own form and deliver it.

When he went to New York to head the BBC office there, Sir Lindsay heard many of Murrow's reports. Years later he noted: "I think I could recognize clearly enough the pattern of mind and the source of things that he had been going into, which produced this finished product." He added that if Murrow made a categorical statement in the course of a broadcast, Sir Lindsay felt that it was indeed true, or at least the odds were very high that it was, "because his research was good, his thinking good."

And Murrow was highly cognizant of his medium. Probably more than anyone else before him, he was aware of "sound" values---that the new medium by which he communicated contained a great deal more for the ear than just one man's voice. He appreciated the kinds of innovations that radio could reflect in different and realistic voices, in sounds of all kinds. It was, and is---as it is called in Britain today---"sound broadcasting."

Referring to the famous Trafalgar Square footsteps report detailed in Alexander Kendrick's *Prime Time*, Sir Lindsay noted how Murrow used sound not just for the sake of sound gimmickry, but for a purpose, for a reason: He deduced a great deal from the pattern of those steps. But this was very much Ed: "Let's be firsthand, let's not just report what somebody said might happen or did happen. I've got to know." That held good for trips over Berlin, or anything else.

Leonard Miall and Robin Duff---of Old Meldrum, near Aberdeen, Scotland---were there at the scene of another unusual broadcast. Miall was bombed out in the third day of the German blitz. For six weeks he lived in one of the safest places in London: the concert hall in Broadcast House, an air-conditioned, steel-reinforced building with corridors and offices ringing the outer edge of it.

Miall was in charge of the BBC's talk programs to Germany. One of the most imaginative broadcasts that Ed did, Miall has noted, was when he took his microphone around that concert hall, just picking up the snores of those of us who were regularly living there. Any producer who had to work evenings, any speaker---including cabinet ministers and other guests who were to do broadcasts in the evening---would be offered a meal and a drink and, after the broadcast, would be bedded down with a mattress and a sheet and pillow. The only stipulation was that the recipient of these blitz-time luxuries was expected to be at Broadcast House by 6:00 p.m. That's when the raids started. In the morning, at the all-clear, everyone could safely go to work.

Robin Duff, who had joined the BBC in 1937 and knew Ed in London early in the war before he went to India, later chuckled with fond recollection of the "snore" broadcast in the concert hall. He remembered Murrow saying, "I must speak softly else I will wake my weary BBC colleagues." And, Duff added, "Ed could get away with this sort of thing." It would seem that John Reith, who had departed to the Ministry of Information at the time, would probably have had his forebodings confirmed about the young broadcaster for CBS. Such informality, personal concern, and description were indeed foreign to the long-established BBC pattern of impersonality and sophistication.

Author and producer D. G. Bridson, in referring to an emerging new kind of radio involving actual sounds, locales, and events, puts it another way: "This was the end of the boiled-shirt tradition in radio. Previously the announcers in their evening dress, waiting to interview the peasantry . . . God!"

CBS officials early in the war suggested some kind of collaborative radio series between the two countries, a program that would alternate weekly, coming one week from America, the next from Britain. Each program would be broadcast simultaneously on the BBC Home Service and on CBS. The idea was to portray the lives of the two peoples, and to emphasize the common strivings of each. Bridson produced the first show when the series began in 1943; Norman Corwin did the first one from America; Bridson was the editor of the series, which lasted three years.

The first program was an "actuality" from the North of England. The theme: What sort of life did the people of Lancashire want after war? The procedure: Pick local people in the area, listen to and record their speech, write a script---using the same words and accents---for them, rehearse and record them in their own homes. Bridson described how he would edit their remarks into script form, rehearse them, correct their mistakes. The wife of one of the characters would listen on the car radio and offer such significant criticism as "no, that's not really Billie." Everyone would volunteer comments, and finally, when the show was produced, "They'd come through like pros," says Bridson.

Murrow had agreed to loan Bob Trout to Bridson, to conduct the North Country interviews. Murrow was delighted with the idea. He knew how much of a novelty plain North Country voices would be to American listeners---irritated as they often were by the London accents of the BBC announcers. In a footnote, Bridson observes how the Beatles, twenty years later, would draw cheers for the same North Country vowels. Murrow confirmed that the idea was unique, that developing a broadcast around ordinary people either in Britain or in the States was simply unheard of.

Three days before the broadcast, Murrow and Bob Trout joined Bridson in the old cotton town of Oldham, in Lancashire. The characters had been chosen and scripted; all that remained were the rehearsals. So for two nights, from blacked-out house to house, the trio would rig up the microphone on the kitchen table, getting everyone used to working with the first American most of them had met. Both Murrow and his hosts were fascinated by the new radio venture, and with each other. Bridson mentioned that they had to eat and drink one sumptuous repast after another, knowing all the while that they were downing perhaps a week's limited rations. Such was the hospitality of the North Country. Bridson also recalls the intense interest with which Murrow conversed with each group. CBS officials howled in dismay at the broadcast, thinking that the BBC's claim that these were everyday ordinary folk was a fraud. Murrow set his company straight. He had been with these people in their homes and in the studio where they gathered for the final production. He explained that they were people talking about what they knew, and had merely been trained to talk in their own words. The fact of the matter was that most British accents, including those of the North Country people, convey a surface impression for Americans of high-level education and general intellectuality.

About a year later, Bridson convinced Murrow to cooperate in bucking the CBS and American radio ban on the use of recordings in broadcasts. He proposed to the CBS director that he transmit a recording of BBC correspondent Stanley Maxted's description of the parachute drop at Arnheim. Bridson said, "I know your ban on recordings; you'll have to cover me on this. I am going to play the recording, and introduce it and then say, 'This is what you're missing!'" The broadcast, recorded live during the intensity of battle with all the accompanying sounds, created much excitement in America, enabling Murrow to say, "If you'd let me do it myself, I could bring you this stuff back anytime!" Such incidents, indeed, contributed to the demise of the outmoded ban.

Bridson knew that Murrow was extremely well informed because he was in touch, directly in touch, with the war cabinet and the services. "Anything that Ed talked about," Bridson has noted, "you knew perfectly well was said after having had dinner the night before with Churchill or somebody. It wasn't a matter of attending news conferences and picking up handouts."

It was also a matter of literally soaking up news, directions, and accounts with contacts at the BBC and, most significantly, with one man, a talented and amusing Scotsman who had been with the *Manchester Guardian*---R. T. Clark. Time and again, Murrow's recollections reflected his close relationship with Clark.

Godfrey Talbot testified to the amount of time Murrow spent with Clark:

> Ed would drift in and out of the newsroom, looking at the tapes, looking at the bulletins, asking questions . . . [and would] spend hour after hour after hour, simply talking, talking with everybody, talking with people in the newsroom, sitting with R. T. Clark, some of it reminiscence, some of it men's smoking-room stories, eternally smoking, gesticulating, pulling out the story.

Talbot's analysis is that Murrow was, without qualification, the supreme newsman when it came to getting the story.

Talbot summarized his views of Murrow the "newsgatherer:"

> L don't think I've ever met a human being who was so single-minded in the pursuit of news as Ed Murrow. He would garner everybody else's opinions and views and experience, but then he would sort it out for himself. He wasn't a man to delegate experience. He had to travel the road by feeling it with his own muscles and his own mind and his own fears and his own nerves. That was my impression of Ed.

Talbot added that the dark night was nightmarish outside during the blitz. Bangs and bumps pounded the London streets into stony debris; and there they were, well-protected in the sub-basement of Broadcast House, sub-editing the news. Ed Murrow had been out on the streets, and he would come into the newsroom late at night, weary, undone; and, as Talbot recalled, "This was the only time I would see him almost naive." Naive? Yes, because one of the impressions Murrow generally gave Talbot was of a professional cynicism. Not a personal cynicism, but a proper professional cynicism, which any good newsman must have to sieve and winnow through the world of news. "But Ed would come in out of the night," Talbot noted, "as touched as a schoolboy with what he had seen in the East End of London or in the streets of London---the firemen, the wardens, the people, the way people were standing up to the bombardment." He'd come back, Talbot thought, as a younger, a simpler man. Here was a hard-bitten newsman, hit in the solar plexus by what he had seen in the streets of London.

The tone of Talbot's remarks was clearly extreme admiration. Another BBC correspondent, Patrick Smith, wrote that he was not quite so impressed by the reactions of Murrow, though he agreed with Talbot about his behavior. Smith said that he knew and admired Murrow during those years in London, "though I thought at the time that he rather overdid the emotion about us brave Londoners who could take it, as the saying went." Smith grew to a different understanding as the years went by because of his own similar experience. It came to him while he was covering the floods of Florence for the BBC many years later: "It dawned on me how a foreign correspondent could feel about other people's sufferings. I realized then, as I did my broadcasts, that I felt about the Florentines as Ed felt about the Londoners." What he felt was a sorrow at their terrible ill luck, "more than matched by the pride in their courageous facing of catastrophe, and overcoming it."

Talbot cautioned against giving the impression of a weeping, crying, theatrical demonstration. But "by golly, Ed was shaken to the core by what he was seeing in London, and, because he was, gave those tremendous broadcasts." In an eloquent summary of how Murrow was able to gather and transmit the significance of events about him, Talbot commented: "Although a hard-bitten man with a hard shell around him, he was a photographic plate. He was a prey to what he saw. This is part of the good newsman's makeup."

To put it another way, Murrow had an "octopus" mind, as former BBC correspondent Howard Marshall remembers him. His mind, Marshall felt, grasped material and never released it until he was on the air.

Frank Gillard and Ed Murrow were in North Africa at the same time, and their travels brought them together on a variety of occasions during the war. Gillard, also a BBC correspondent, retired as head of BBC radio services so as to undertake various consulting, research, and writing projects, among which has been that of consultant with the United States Corporation for Public Broadcasting.

Gillard, in one of his recent communications, wrote of Murrow preparing a broadcast back in those war days:

> My recollection is of a man who went through agonies of concentration to write his story. He sat over his typewriter, enveloped and isolated in clouds of cigarette smoke, oblivious to all around him. He really worked at his story, concerned both to relate an accurate narrative and to point up its significance.

That's almost precisely the way Michael Balkwill tells it: "He'd go over to a quiet typewriter in a quiet corner and you'd see him start to knock out his dispatch." Occasionally he'd look up and ask a question about the British reaction to the bombing or whatever. Then he'd return to his typewriter and his cigareete, and he'd rattle out a few more lines, and drift away with that.

Balkwill also confirms that a great deal of what went into those Murrow scripts was the result of much conversation and talk with those in the newsroom: "He used to look into our newsroom a very great deal, not only to find the news at its source, but he would talk to everybody in the newsroom." And he'd ask questions: "I always felt he attached considerable importance to this as a cross-section of opinion about the news at the time."

More than any other person in the newsroom, it was the commanding presence of the Scots news editor, R. T. Clark, that attracted Murrow. Certainly part of the bond between them---and it was great, Michael Balkwill felt---was the fact that Clark, a considerable student of German affairs, was on the Nazi blacklist. "Ed had a very great regard for R. T.'s opinions on the news of the day, and what was going to happen, and particularly for his learning and scholarship."

Balkwill says that Clark was a thorough scholar and often illustrated his points with references to classical or medieval history. This used to interest Ed Murrow very much indeed. Balkwill was in the newsroom throughout the war, and has recalled with some nostalgia those long evenings of talk:

> These conversations would go on far into the night in the editor's room in Broadcasting House. I should like to have tape recordings of these conversations, with war noises going on outside, with these two people talking and other people who happened to be there joining in, with this curious mixture of the past and present, the knowledge of what war was about, what power was about, what dangers, ... [These were] very moving occasions.

When asked if, in other words, there was a grappling with theoretical questions as well as the daily news, Balkwill replied:

> Yes, very much, overlaid of course with direct questions: 'R. T., what are the Axis going to do in North Africa?' This kind of thing. He'd say,

> 'Well, Brother [he often used this typically American greeting in conversations], for my money . . . .' interspersed with funny stories on both sides. Bacon sandwiches would be sent for, at the very small hours, 2:30 or 3:30 in the morning. What is important is the importance that Ed Murrow attached to this kind of conversation.
>
> Why? I think, because in his professional role, here were the British professionals in his own profession, at work, under fire, and they were people whose knowledge of events I think he found useful not only in framing broadcasts he was doing, but also in stimulating ideas of his own; it was a cross-fertilizing process; he certainly stimulated his listeners by what he said.

These late-night conversations would sometimes move from Clark's office to a nearby canteen, or to the Hallam Street flat nearby. Perhaps, after the all-clear, Murrow would suggest a bourbon at the flat where the talk would continue, including readings. He'd read some Thurber short stories to the group, and very capably, Balkwill felt. "Perhaps dawn would be breaking, broken glass in the street; you felt this really was a great moment to be alive with a great man---that's what I'd feel."

There are many aspects of Murrow's character and work that Balkwill remembered, but the most significant one was

> his outgoingness, his wish and ability to talk with people, to communicate, to know what they were thinking. He was interested in what people thought and what they felt.
>
> He'd be interested in anything that interested anybody else. If you'd said, 'I always played chess during the blitz,' then Ed would either say, 'Oh, you play chess too. Have you tried the opening gambit of . . . .' or 'I've never played chess. Why did you play chess during the blitz? Do you find it soothing? Or stimulating?'
>
> This is what I mean about his interest in people and what they were thinking and feeling.

Balkwill cited a personal example. He once sent Murrow a picture of his son catching a fish. A reply was soon forthcoming in which Murrow wrote, perhaps with more than just a touch of reminiscence on the part of the one-time rancher and woodsman, that these really were the important things.

Throughout his reminiscence, Balkwill stressed again and again the interest that Ed Murrow had in people. Not in any manipulative sense of "using" people. It was a genuine interest in people---an exploring and a searching-out, as a kind of input for his own outgoing communication with his audience. "If I had to put it in one sentence," Balkwill commented, "it would be about his wish to communicate with other people, and his ability to communicate what he had learned to his audience."

For a more direct view of the way Murrow functioned in his capacity as reporter and news-gatherer, we can look to a member of that wartime staff. London was, and is, familiar ground to CBS correspondent Charles Collingwood. He was with Murrow in London throughout the war years. His base of operations in recent years has also been there, in the modest headquarters of CBS News on Brompton Road, across from the famous Harrods' Department Store. It was there, one cool spring day in 1971 that Collingwood talked about his former boss.

Collingwood stressed that the desk and Murrow were not congenial companions. It is in the nature of the work that a certain amount of time must be consumed at the desk, because it is imperative that the reporter read the literature of his profession, which begins with the newspapers and then includes everything else that's written about what you're going to talk about: politics, military art, progress of the war, and all the rest. So it was that Murrow could not escape the office.

"Ed always felt chained down by the necessities of broadcasting from the studio," Collingwood continued.

> He always wanted to get out into the field. All through the war, he envied those correspondents who could get away for long periods of time. And he himself did what he could, which in the beginning of the war meant going on bombing raids. . . .
> This was something he could do, and then be back in a reasonably short time. Even strict orders from William Paley, the principal executive officer of CBS, could not keep him out of planes, ships, villages, or the streets of London.

Collingwood voiced the opinion that Murrow's lack of education and training in journalism was of no particular moment in carrying out his task: "I don't think the lack of journalistic training made any difference to any of us. I went to the best journalism school in the world---the United Press." But Murrow was just as well-prepared for his job:

> He had the instincts of a reporter; that is, curiosity, attention to facts and detail, and the ability to express himself succinctly and indeed epigrammatically--- which, in the short compass of a radio broadcast, is essential.

Murrow's past did prepare him for his entrance into the broadcaster's world; he had several contacts in Austria, from his student days, and his work with the Institute of International Education. When he assumed the job of Director of Talks, a decided change in emphasis occurred. Most of the programs became truly "talks" and were mostly news-oriented. Commented Collingwood: "It was the most natural thing in the world for him to begin broadcasting with a story breaking under his feet. From that grew the regular European service." Meanwhile, in New York the early patterns of CBS broadcasts were being established by Paul White with the blessings of the CBS hierarchy.

Because of the time difference, Murrow would start his working day---officially, that is, as he may have been up all night in Clark's office---late in the morning, coming into the office about 10:00 or 10:30 to check out news sources and possibilities and start building his broadcast, which would be delivered in the late evening for dinner-time transmission from New York. Again, Collingwood lends credence to the widespread and important associations Murrow had in London: "He had the most enormous range of contacts and friends among people of all walks of life, from the top on down. Churchill conceived great regard for him. When Gil Winant was our ambassador here, he and Ed were very close."

Murrow covered his beat thoroughly around the city, according to Collingwood, and he did indeed enjoy the Commons debates. The play of British politics fascinated him, and some of the formalities also fascinated him. He was very impressed with the caliber of debate in the House. He could quote you marvelous bits of Churchill, or Nye Bevin, or Bob Boothby, or some of the other people who could get up on their feet in the House of Commons and dash off a marvelous epigram. The rhetoric and interplay of British political life were significant for the former college debater. Nor was the parliamentary system played down in his hierarchy of values. He referred to the maintenance of the British government's procedures of parliamentary debate as one of the more significant victories coming out of the war.

When he prepared his broadcasts, Murrow was very much aware that they were meant to be spoken and listened to, rather than read. A tape machine was available in the office even in the war days, and he would work with it. As for preparing the actual newscast, he did not---as Balkwill and others indicated---always type his script in the quiet confines of his own thinking amid the chaos of the newsroom. He frequently dictated his broadcasts to his secretary, Kay Campbell. "I thought that this was remarkable," Collingwood said, "and I used to try to pattern myself on Ed. I felt if . . . well, if this is the way a great broadcaster does it, then I'll try to do it." It was a failure. Collingwood soon discovered that when he dictated a broadcast, it took even more time to recast it and scratch it up with a pencil afterwards to make sense of it than to sit down at a typewriter and grind it out at the beginning. "I've never been able to dictate something and find it usable. But Ed was," he concluded.

Were the dictated scripts always a finished product? Collingwood admitted that of course Ed would have to edit the scripts. He'd scratch up his spoken copy, give it back to whatever girl was preparing it, and she would type up a clean copy. "Once in a while, he'd make some scribbles on those [final copies], as does anyone in broadcasting. But his first draft---and often quite a complete one---was ad-libbed." Collingwood said that Murrow was a marvelous ad-libber in those days. Robin Duff disagreed with

with this appraisal, although he was not nearly so familiar with Murrow's work. Duff said that he could not imagine Murrow as a good ad-libber, just picking up a running commentary, although he felt Murrow was an excellent stylist. Duff was more impressed with Murrow as an interviewer, claiming he was "subtle," whereas "interviewers today browbeat people." Murrow's ad-libbing, according to Collingwood, was "always very clean. Not full of the oh's and ah's and um's and hesitations the rest of us used."

Collingwood's answer to the question of what makes a good ad-libber was instructive and insightful into the talent of Ed Murrow:

> I think, to be a good ad-libber, you have to be well schooled in the construction of an English sentence, and be habituated to speaking in complete sentences. Secondly, you must have an orderly mind. Thirdly, you must have some kind of very rapid connection between the eye, the brain, and the tongue. In some people it's more rapid than others. So in some sense I suppose it's a gift. Ed had all those things.

Unless there was a particularly hideous bombing raid on London he wanted to talk about, Murrow would prepare his broadcasts before dinner and come in later for the 11:00 or 11:15 newscast. Most of the news of the day was in by 8:00 p.m. He would come in after the evening meal, and immediately check the wires to make sure there hadn't been some new development that was more important than the one he had prepared for his delivery. On other occasions, he'd eat first and come in and do the entire broadcast preparation after dinner. Kay Campbell, his secretary, would also come in and assist with the work. Because of the blitz, people had to get home, so restaurants closed fairly early, allowing the evening for either writing the script, covering some aspect of the blitz, or whatever.

There were some stories, Charles Collingwood felt, that Murrow just didn't attempt to do, or did not do well, although of course he was a general reporter:

> He was never very good with the humorous broadcast and had sense enough not to try. Very few people are any good at that. If he told an anecdote, it was always because it had some meaning, not because it was funny or amusing.

He particularly liked to report on action, such as the bombing raids or the effect of the blitz in London. And he particularly enjoyed the sort of "analytical" pieces which one could do when newscasts were frequently fifteen minutes long.

"But Ed's best broadcasts, and the thing I think he liked best to do," Collingwood has noted, "were always related to some aspect of reality that he had seen or personally experienced." It was the difference, Collingwood felt, between an abstract painter and one whose painting is always anchored in some image of reality. Added Collingwood: "Ed was not too good, nor did he greatly enjoy, abstract kinds of broadcasts and analyses. His were always like a painting related to something that he had seen and gone through."

Collingwood stressed that Murrow could generalize and make deductions from the specifics on which he was reporting, but not spin great theories. From Collingwood's perspective, "Ed would have been, for instance, a very poor Kremlinologist, who deduces from who is photographed in the May Day parade, in what order, what the inner workings of the Kremlin are." It was Collingwood's assessment that Murrow's best work involved reporting some reality that he had seen or personally experienced. If he had been there, his nerve endings and his total perception were so much sharper, so much clearer.

Edward R. Murrow never felt comfortable at a desk, and only at the twilight of his career and his life was he restricted to it. He had to cover the story, he had to be there, and almost any part of covering a story in wartime meant some kind of danger. It was sought by him. Danger seemed to harbor an attraction for him. All of Ed's wartime colleagues, somewhere in their conversations about his London career, mentioned Ed Murrow's "bravery." His brave deeds made possible the kind of reporting he did. Bravery and action were normal but integral parts of Murrow's collecting of data to be broadcast home.

A communications expert might pose the question: Was being at the scene a necessary part of the job? Did he endanger his life to cover actions partly from a guilty conscience because he was personally not involved in the fight against Nazi Germany? Or was it much more mysterious and hidden than that? Was it part of some strange psychological need, unrelated to war and war coverage? These are questions that might provide links to the work and character of Ed Murrow. There are, of course, no definite answers. One can present only a sample of reaction from those who knew him and worked with him.

Tom Barman simply felt that the core of Murrow's being was "action." Murrow, he felt, wanted to do things, to get things moving. He compared Murrow, as a man of action more than words, to Winston Churchill, another master of action and words. Perhaps, in addition to political factors, the respect which these two men held for each other was partly the unspoken recognition of a common bond of inner traits.

Richard Marriott recalled an "odd episode" involving himself, Fred Bate (NBC's representative early in the war), and Murrow. "Fred and Ed decided to go and watch the blitz, not inside London, but at a fighter airdrome in Essex, at Hornchurch on the estuary." He said that they had spent the night there, had eaten dinner in a little inn and slept in a haystack, watching the aircraft and lights. Then they had driven on to Dover. Concluded Fred: "Ed wanted always to be where there were guns firing. Dover was being shelled. We had lunch in Dover. Why? And why together, I just don't know."

Later, Marriott resigned from the BBC and himself became a night fighter. He was a navigator and was stationed in Essex, but he maintained a flat on Devon Street in London where he would spend a forty-eight-hour leave whenever he could. Commented Marriott:

> I had read about Ed doing this Berlin flight. I was much impressed. Bomber chaps had it much harder than we did. You [fighters] were on the hunting end, not the hunted end.

He went to visit the Murrows at their Hallam Street flat, but they were out, so he left a note instead which read: "I wouldn't do a thing like that unless under military orders. Jolly good show." Later, Marriott received a letter from Ed in which he responded, "It's given me more pleasure hearing from someone in the Air Force saying this, than all the cheers in Fleet Street pubs."

Was Murrow especially pleased by an indication of equality with those who had to fight? Perhaps so. Cecilia Reeves, in commenting about his Berlin air raid jaunts, said that he felt he had to make those flights as a matter of principle. "He told me," she said,

> 'My doing that won't win the war, but it will be lost if people like me don't do their job. The fact that I'm flying over Berlin won't win the war, but the fact that people like me do not share the experience will not win the war, or keep the peace afterward.'

Another occasion involving personal danger occurred late in the year of the blitz---1941. Marriott, along with Eric Sevareid, recalled later how Murrow faced a dramatic and immediate threat to their safety. Murrow had invited Marriott to meet Sevareid at the Langham Hotel, next to Broadcast House. A small bomb hit the hotel. "It sounded terrible," Marriott vividly recalls, "a tremendous great crack, and everyone wanted to dive underneath the table. Ed didn't pay any attention at all, kept on eating, and said, 'Someone must have dropped something up there.'" When asked if Murrow didn't at least flinch, Marriott said, "Not at all. No, he was as cold as ice, really, about this. Whether this was immense courage or whether it was a sort of toughness of fibre, an insensitivity to danger, he certainly had it."

Marriott said that Murrow actually seemed to seek out danger with his flight over Berlin and other such adventures, because all correspondents felt it was wrong not to be fighting:

> I'm sure Ed had this feeling, too. I think this was a compensation in a way for not being in the war. . . . A good journalist has these guts. If you're frightened by temperament, you have to overcome it some way. I don't think he was frightened by temperament.

Was he more courageous than other American reporters? Concluded Marriott: "I would think more than almost anybody. I think he had a tremendous coolness in the face of danger."

Eric Sevareid remembers it this way:

> I was in the lobby talking to some Australian girl, late at night. He was around in the dining room, which was almost empty, talking to somebody from the BBC [presumably Marriott]. And WHAM, things hit the top. Plaster started to pour through; water poured through the roof. People coming down in their bathrobes, heading for the shelters. I went around that long corridor into the dining room. He was sitting there talking.
> I said, 'Ed, I think we've been hit.'
> He was rather annoyed with me. He said, 'No, that's at least as far away as Oxford Circus.' But we had been in his office. His office, which was in a little building adjoining his hotel, was hit too. It was put out. It was the first American office knocked out in London by the bombing. The next morning we went up there and it was a total mess. Bill Paley's picture hanging by one wire, plaster all over his desk, glass, all the windows broken. We had to move out.

When asked if Murrow had been annoyed that Sevareid had brought it to his attention, Sevareid replied: "I guess so. He thought I was being nervous, or . . . I don't know. We *had* been hit. He realized that in a few moments."

Writing in *Not So Wild a Dream* a quarter of a century later, Sevareid recalled another episode when Murrow stood on a rooftop with a young British bomber pilot who had flown over Berlin many times, but had never before been under bombing. The young man was shaken and appalled, and said that he had never dreamed it was like this. He wanted only to get away from London to the safety of his machine. Sevareid continued:

> After a while most of us came to feel that our margin of protective behavior was so small as to be almost nonexistent, that whether we lived or died was a matter that we could do very little about. A few strong souls like Murrow found a certain release in that, I think. On me it had a depressive effect for some time.

Sevareid then told of the oft-repeated speculation as to whether there might be some sort of "mysterious sense" within a person that perceives impending disaster. He, Murrow, and CBS newsman Larry Lesueur were walking outside the BBC and around to the side of Broadcast House. Nothing was heard, but suddenly, without any hint of the reason for his behavior, Murrow jumped into a doorway. "Larry and I immediately followed suit. At that moment a jagged casing from an anti-aircraft shell crashed precisely where we had been."

Sevareid's reference to Murrow as one who found a "release" in dangerous circumstances is confirmed and amplified by others who knew him. There is unanimous agreement, among his colleagues, for example, that Ed Murrow loved speed and always drove his car rapidly. He had a fascination with movement and action.

Former BBC staffer and writer Herbert Agar, said that he was not close to Murrow, but nevertheless saw him frequently in London during the war years. He stated flatly that Murrow simply loved danger and, in fact, had to have it to survive. "It was a drug without which he felt deflated." As a result, he constantly and illegally got aboard planes scheduled to fly over Germany. Herbert Agar recalled one episode which suggests that beneath the rational level of needing to cover the story, to experience it, there was a psychological factor that in fact compelled Murrow to participate in these raids:

> One day (was it 1943?) I made a bet in the Saville Club that I could tell the next time Ed had broken all rules and had been on one of these terrifying (to me) flights. I could tell, I bet, because he would be so much more agreeable, so much less of a denigrator of all men's hopes. I won the bet. Ed was always at his best when the bombs were falling or he had broken all the rules to go aloft and have another look at death.

Thomas Barman attributed the same psychological bent to Churchill, who slept the best when the news was the worst.

Sir Lindsay Wellington did not attach any mysterious significance to this desire for action and danger, but he seemed to believe that action and danger were indeed a tonic for Ed Murrow. Maybe he was reckless. Certainly Murrow was not a desk man, Sir Lindsay felt; the time would simply arrive "when he had enough of the desk, and needed, if you like, the refreshment of action. To hell with the danger. This was a counterbalancing need of his nature, I would think."

The question of whether Murrow possessed a death wish has been raised by Alexander Kendrick and others. It is a presumptuous and complex question to answer. The raising of the question, however, obviously stemmed from something in the behavior of Murrow that was observed by his associates.

"No question of a death wish," replied Sir Lindsay, when queried on the matter; "but he was certainly brave and courageous. Never mind the great spectacular things of flying about the place." He then pointed out that to tell the story of the British reaction to bombing, to sharpen his judgment and give it a firmer perspective, Ed had to get out into the streets to feel what it was like to be bombed.

Eric Sevareid was uncertain of the "death wish" theory, but firm on the question of Murrow's bravery: "He had, some of his friends thought, a kind of death wish about him; I don't know. I wouldn't go that far." But Sevareid also added that his former employer "had this thing about speed. He knew that. He'd talk about that more than once. He loved speeds, high speeds. It gave him some kind of thrill."

There was nothing abnormal about Murrow's sense of reality in a situation of fear, according to Sevareid. While people often refer to Murrow's "cool" reaction to danger, Sevareid insisted that Murrow was aware of the adverse conditions. "He was truly a a brave man, because he was scared to death half the time and he'd still do it!"

Sevareid elaborated on the concept of bravery in wartime as it related to Ed Murrow:

> That's what guts is. If you're not scared. . . . I knew Medal of Honor winners in the war. One or two, Army psychiatrists would explain to you, simply had no sense of fear. They were not brave men; they were not normal men! Ed was perfectly normal in this. He could be plenty scared, but he wouldn't show it. What he was afraid of was being afraid!
>
> Now, Hemingway had some of this same fixation about physical bravery. There must be much deeper reasons for this. Because Ed would not go into shelters. I thought he was crazy not to. He took these damn risks. And he told me once, 'Well, I don't go into a shelter, because if I started doing it I'm afriad I might not stop.'
>
> He was afraid of himself. And therefore he did things that I thought foolish. But somehow, they gave him confidence.

Michael Standing stressed Murrow's bravery, and the fact that you would find him in the "exposed positions" during the blitz. Standing described, almost poetically, the huge fire raids when the sky would light up like dawn, and the city was a mass of light. "During one really bad one when St. Paul's was set aflame, I can't recall exactly where Ed was, but I'm quite sure his visage was lit up by flames somewhere."

"Ed was as cool as a cucumber," recalled Michael Balkwill. "A bomb did go off in Broadcast House once during the nine o'clock news. Once we had to evacuate the newsroom. His presence would be one reason for making you feel a bit more at ease during a rough night." He was, said Balkwill, "unflappable."

Ed Murrow was a brave man. Whatever the sources of his bravery, and its ultimate meaning, it played a part in his accomplishments as a reporter. But more than that, his bravery was a continuing source of support for his friends and colleagues who together were undertaking somewhat of a revolution in "broadcast journalism" under dangerous and sometimes terrifying conditions. Ed Murrow's courage and strength lent support to that common effort.

CHAPTER V

THE BBC MILIEU AND INFLUENCE

In performing his tasks, Murrow did not operate in a vacuum. He had come to his new undertaking of wartime reporter and observer unprepared, in a technical sense, to perform the task. As already noted, Collingwood observed that, for himself, the best "training school" in journalism was the United Press, although he had had formal training and education in journalism.

Ed Murrow had no such training. The closest he came to it was in his debate and speech work with Ida Lou Anderson at Washington State College (That poignant story of learning and devotion is discussed in Alexander Kendrick's *Prime Time*.) Yet even that was "merely a little frosting on the cake," according to CBS news commentator Richard Hottelet. He had a naturally pleasant voice quality, and the education to use it. As Hottelet said, that had nothing to do with preparing Murrow as a reporter, however, with the exception of the issue orientation and skill in argument arising out of his debate work. So he began as a reporter with a background of administration, travel, an insatiable curiosity, and a reservoir of untapped potential as a commentator.

The first news organization that Edward R. Murrow worked with professionally was the BBC. He worked *through* and *around* the organization, and *with* its personnel. He did not, however, work *for* the BBC, although he appeared on many of its programs.

During these developing years in which he was both learning and directing---and evolving---his new job, the BBC obviously made an impression on him about what news is, how to gather it, and what to do with it. It is clear that Murrow's commitment on his own broadcast system with its form of private ownership was supportive during these years, though this was to change much later in his career.

From his many experiences with the BBC, the question emerged as to what influences the BBC had had on Murrow, if any; and, in return, the question is similarly posed as to whether Murrow affected the BBC organization, and in what ways. There are no definitive answers, but some strong suggestions that can contribute to a greater understanding of Murrow's work in later years.

Sir Lindsay Wellington was emphatic in stating that no direct control over Murrow's operation was ever exercised by the BBC:

> The impact of the BBC wasn't in any sense to change by one word or letter what he was saying, what he was doing. . . . We lent [CBS] a studio, mikes and engineers and things to do with his own job. He wasn't beholden to us in any kind of way which would modify that at all.

But Sir Lindsay felt that there was a lot that Murrow liked about British broadcasting. He thought it sensible, for example, to use broadcasting as a social instrument, that is, as an instrument for serving "all sorts and conditions of people." As for a *commercial* system of broadcasting? Sir Lindsay spoke less convincingly at first, but still added: "He [Murrow] wasn't necessarily bound to the thought that it was best to use it as an advertising medium." Reflecting further on the point, he added: "He valued human values and human qualities more than quantities of advertising."

The relationship with the BBC seemed to be a highly compatible one, but in a nonarticulated way. It was just a natural thing. Or, as Sir Lindsay observed: "Congenitally, I think he and the BBC were thinking along roughly similar lines." According to Michael Standing, the BBC acted as a friend and confidant:

> I suppose he gained something through working with us. I think the very willingness of the BBC to accept him as part of themselves, more or less, to involve his participation in some of *our* broadcasts as well as our participation in many of his, was an indication that we really were as one.

Leonard Miall, who served the BBC in various capacities for over thirty years, expressed the relationship in a way that left little room for doubt that the BBC's influence on Murrow was considerable: "I think it influenced him a very great deal. Because he was living here, he was listening to BBC news all the time."

Frank Gillard, former BBC war correspondent, stressed the personal rapport: "I felt as if I was talking to a BBC colleague. In fact, I always considered that the BBC was Ed's true spiritual home." Both the BBC and Murrow held the same philosophy of broadcasting, Gillard felt, and by implication said that it was simply mutual reinforcement. It may or may not have been a matter of the philosophy of a powerful broadcasting organization seeping into the spirit and work of a gifted but untrained newsman. It may rather have been just a fortunate coming together of like-minded approaches at the outset.

On the other hand, Michael Balkwill felt that perhaps there was a more direct influence on Murrow than that attributable to initial rapport: "The BBC may have played some part in what he put into his own work, at a time when these values were at a discount in most other broadcasting organizations in the world." Murrow's values, Balkwill said, were simply summed up in the BBC's policy of objective and accurate reporting. Thus, even in a direct way, as was pointed out earlier, Murrow used the BBC personnel for sources of his own thought, analysis, and inspiration, as indeed the BBC utilized his talents in their programs.

One of the most eloquent statements to emerge from countless interviews in England about the relationships between the BBC and Ed Murrow came from Godfrey Talbot, a husky, energetic former BBC official. In semi-retirement, Talbot conveyed the impression of one who was busy savoring all the remaining moments of life. I was grateful for the brief time we spent together in 1971 in a quickly requisitioned office in the back of Broadcast House.

Sitting back in his chair between appointments, he rapidly described a man whom he obviously loved very much: "Everyone regarded him as part of the outfit here, not simply because the BBC gave him the facilities, but because Ed fitted in!" His fuller statement is worth recording for its insights:

> It wasn't the case of this is a chap from the other side of the Atlantic, and, you know, he's a curious fish, and we're curious fish.
> He didn't talk as we talked. Many of his habits were not our own habits, but he was immediately accepted and acceptable. This was his home. He lived in this place.

As for how Murrow felt about the BBC:

> I think he had an admiration, of course, for what was being done in British broadcasting. I think that he found, the BBC person, all kinds, not one type, but he found many of them entertaining; we may have been figures of fun to some degree.
> But everything was grist for Ed's mill, you see. All life, . . . there was nothing that he didn't want to savor in life, I think, and in people.
> In the BBC, I think he found a world very different from his own world. We professionally . . . had the same yardsticks, and the same practice in news, but we were essentially a different people. We didn't, for one thing, cut through barriers and forms and styles, and antecedents and pre-selected forms as he did.

And, apparently, the BBC did teach Murrow a few things, at least by way of emphasis, according to Talbot:

> I think possibly he learned from the BBC something of what we thought, rightly I think, was our own rather stern objectivity; our news division's over-anxiety, if you like, to make the news absolutely objective and without personal flavor. As you know, the BBC would give the news starkly and with its full badness when things were going badly, and therefore, when there was good news to tell, that good news was believed because we told the bad news with frankness.
> All this, of course, appealed to Ed enormously. He was never one to cover up, to dissemble, to make a jolly picture, to build up a small incident out of proportion. He had this passion for integrity and stark narration.
> He wanted to get down to the bare bones, always, and I think we were doing the same thing. He therefore found---a silly phrase---professional soul-mates in the BBC.

In spite of differences, Murrow and the BBC were traveling the same path, Talbot explained:

> We were very British; he was very American, at least to us he was. We sounded different, and our behavior was different, our gestures and performances. But we were traveling the same road, and he found he was in the right stable.
>
> Not necessarily the BBC in general; he wasn't concerned with the BBC in general, but with news in particular, and we were up the same street.
>
> I think he was always glad to know that within this mammoth organization, this public corporation, there was this hard core of news efficiency, not only Broadcast House, but in the BBC's output generally.

Godfrey Talbot ultimately summed up the relationship between the BBC and Ed Murrow, as he saw it, in just one short sentence: "In the halls of Broadcast House, the name of Ed Murrow is there in gold, and he was one of us."

Murrow's colleague, Charles Collingwood, agreed with the Talbot view of BBC policy and its impact on the young Murrow, as indeed on CBS itself. "I think the idea of how you handle news was very much influenced by the BBC," he said. "The BBC decided that its credibility as an international broadcasting service depended on its reliability and the truth and fairness with which it treated matters."

But Collingwood asserted that this influence was only one of strong reinforcement, not a new concept. "Now this, as an ideal, was always Ed's; it was also Paley's; it remains that of CBS news; I think it remains that of broadcast news in general. And some of that came from the BBC." And Collingwood felt also that Murrow applied that philosophy to the end of his career:

> He carried that on, you know, when he was in USIA, insisting successfully that the American overseas broadcasts, sponsored by the government, should show the shadows as well as the bright spots and the faults as well as the glories of American civilization.

Richard Dimbleby---the BBC's Edward R. Murrow

One cannot spend any amount of time in England without becoming aware that Britain had its own Edward R. Murrow; perhaps it is instructive to take at least a brief look here at the parallels between the two men, the effect of the Englishman on the BBC and, indirectly, his effect on Murrow.

Certainly the philosophy of the BBC was shaped to some degree by a young man on Fleet Street, who wrote a letter to the Corporation in May of 1936 while Murrow was still Director of

Talks, not yet having assumed the role of CBS European Director. In that letter, 22-year-old Richard Dimbleby suggested that the BBC institute the idea of "on-the-spot" broadcasters to report on events, rather than rely on just an agency report of the event. Dimbleby justified this position in stating that "There can be no vital authority on a sudden news event, unless it be the man in the street who was on the spot." Dimbleby went on to suggest how to prepare the complete newscast:

> The description of the event, in addition to the story written by the reporter and any agency matter which you may care to use, could be transmitted from the studio, to which your representative could bring the eye-witness.

This approach to broadcasting is so commonplace today in any radio or television newscast that perhaps it seems trivial to record the thought. At the time, in what was then a staid and sedate Corporation, in a world that hardly knew the potentialities of electronic journalism, the idea could be described as revolutionary.

But to Dimbleby the idea wasn't so new. As Fleet Street's youngest editor (new editor of the *Advertiser's Weekly*), he declared that a precedent had been set by "newspaper newsreels." By this he said he meant that

> this principle of enlivening news by the infusion of the human element is being followed in other spheres. The method followed is that of not only showing the news, but telling why and how it happened. That is what I suggest the BBC could do with great success, not only with sudden events or catastrophes, but with all types of news.

The BBC, in its slow, careful, conservative way of adjusting, took its time about young Dimbleby. Months passed before anything happened. And Dimbleby had tried before; his letter referred to an earlier job interview. In September, 1936, however, the BBC took him on in a rather minor position of Topical Talks Assistant.

Unlike Murrow, Dimbleby's relationship to journalism was passed on to him by his antecedents. His grandfather, F. W. Dimbleby, had acquired a group of local newspapers at Richmond in Surrey. His father had worked in Fleet Street for much of his life. And throughout much of his own life, Richard managed the Richmond papers.

When war came, he joined the growing number of news correspondents for the BBC. While he and Murrow knew each other, met each other, their separate but parallel careers did not intersect for long periods of time. Dimbleby was in France during the "phony war," while Murrow was working in London. While Murrow reported the blitz, Dimbleby was in the Middle East. Dimbleby covered the invasion of Europe, while Murrow kept at his post in England. Both visited Germany's concentration camps at about the same time at the war's end.

Murrow's reputation was greater in Britain, in those days, than Dimbleby's seemed to be. While doing an excellent job of reporting from the various fronts, Dimbleby was one of many BBC colleagues doing the same thing. One can only wonder as to what extent Murrow looked in Dimbleby's direction for guidance in evaluating his own work.

About the time that Murrow became a CBS executive after the war, Dimbleby resigned from the BBC as a regular news announcer-reporter. He was somewhat miffed that that was all the BBC could offer him. He knew that he had more to contribute.

After resigning, Dimbleby went back to his newspaper work, took reporting assignments from time to time, and then blossomed into a name reporter with his documentary program "Panorama," that became a regular weekly documentary on the BBC. This program was evolving as Murrow was returning to the air and commencing his own documentaries, "Hear It Now" and "See It Now." Dimbleby turned, as did Murrow, to the non-news side of television. Murrow became popular with "Person to Person," Dimbleby with "Twenty Questions." Dimbleby, again like Murrow, continued to report on major state occasions, coronations, elections, and other on-the-spot events as well as "Panorama," almost to the time of his death.

Both men possessed a high degree of communicative ability and keen perception in covering events. Such words as "integrity," "courage," and "dedication" are used in describing both of them. In a professional sense, many of the key attributes discussed in this book could apply to either man.

Of course there were many personal and private differences between the two, as well as some professional ones. In the first place, they were quite different physically. Dimbleby more nearly resembled a defensive linebacker for a professional football team---tall, heavy, and physically rugged; Murrow was tall but lean, more traditionally handsome, scholarly in appearance. While Murrow certainly had a wry, though subdued, sense of humor, Dimbleby was more prone to the belly laugh. He was a "jolly" man in the American sense of the word. In fact, one might, on first viewing each man, mistake the American for the Englishman and the Englishman for the American, if one had had little experience with the English and were only reacting to stereotypes.

There lives culminated tragically. Each man died in the same year, of the same disease. Dimbleby had fought off the ravages of cancer for five years. Though the malignancy first appeared in his back in 1960, he managed to work nearly to the end, leading a productive and successful life.

When Ed Murrow died and Dimbleby took part in the BBC memorial tributes to him, it must have been an agonizing task. Leonard Miall described Dimbleby's tribute as an act of great courage because Dimbleby himself was in great physical pain---and certainly must also have suffered emotional pain as well, for he knew that he would soon meet a similar fate.

Within two months of Dimbleby's death, Leonard Miall brought out a book on him, published by the BBC. It was dedicated to Richard Dimbleby "in gratitude for the standards he set and the courage he showed." The book recorded his long career, the major stories that Dimbleby covered, the scripts of key broadcasts, and recollections of his colleagues. The book was entitled simply *Richard Dimbleby Broadcaster*.[1]

Following in his father's footsteps, Richard Dimbleby's son, David, a serious-appearing young man, has broadcast a BBC evening program called "Twenty-Four Hours," in which the news is analyzed and probed with various guests. Young David Dimbleby was part of a controversy involving that program that erupted in June of 1971 when he interviewed former Prime Minister Harold Wilson on a segment entitled "Yesterday's Men." Questions by Dimbleby about Wilson's finances produced a protest to the BBC by the Labor Party's leader, which led to a major investigation into the matter. Although generally operating free from direct governmental controls, the BBC has, from time to time, been forced to defend its "objectivity" and "nonpartisanship" from such attacks.

Rather than attempting to explore the specific influences that Richard Dimbleby had on Ed Murrow's style or work, it might be sufficient to note that the early careers of both men evolved in the same organizational environment---the BBC. Certainly, Dimbleby's new ideas on reporting for the electronic media were first developed and utilized in a sophisticated manner by the British Broadcasting Corporation. Other men, including Ed Murrow, brought similar ideas to fruition. The later parallel nature of their careers reflects a kind of thinking and approach that typified the BBC operation over those earlier years and tended to condition the thinking and styles of both men.

Finally, it should be noted that one man pursued his work through a public noncommercial system, whereas the other functioned primarily within a commercial system. Integrity and a high level of journalistic professionalism operated in both systems. In retrospect, it appears that what Dimbleby was to the BBC, Murrow was to CBS. And both broadcasting systems were much the better for it.

---

[1] Leonard Miall, ed. (by his colleagues), *Richard Dimbleby Broadcaster* (London: British Broadcasting Corporation, 1966).

CHAPTER VI

A PHILOSOPHY OF REPORTING

Murrow did not write a treatise on his emerging profession. But he did reveal---in various interviews, short articles, conversations with others, and broadcasts---the basic ideas on which his philosophy of broadcast journalism was based. Others who knew Murrow or worked with him have also been able to contribute insights about how he viewed his job during that early formative period in England.

One can start with an early glimpse of Murrow's philosophy of communications at the age of twenty-seven. At that time, August, 1935, he was interviewed by L. Marsland Gander, the radio correspondent for the London *Daily Telegraph*. In the article, Gander described his visit to the BBC and to other countries to survey problems involved in Murrow's new job. Gander reported that Murrow had some original ideas of transatlantic talks that would involve, *inter alia*, an exchange of common experiences in common professions in the two countries. A New York "cop" and a London "bobby," or a New York subway attendant and a London Underground worker, for example, might compare their daily lives in a transAtlantic dialogue. Other suggested ideas would include conversations between two friends, talking across the Atlantic about everything from weekends at Brighton to politics in both countries. Such conversations could be transcribed and broadcast by the BBC as well as by the Columbia System.

Reporter Gander continued: "Programmes from Europe have been hitherto something of a 'stunt' in American programmes. In the future, Mr. Murrow would like to work talks from England into a general scheme." Murrow's intentions were to maintain a balance between the two main political parties, and to give adequate representation to minorities. In short, the story reported what Murrow was to tell the somewhat perturbed broadcast elitist John Reith of the BBC two years later. Two principles should prevail: (1) people with "common" experiences would share their ideas and reactions, and the programs would involve a variety of "common" people; and, (2) debate and discussion over major public issues would, however, comprise the content of many of these talks. In discussing the prospective programs, Murrow repeatedly expressed concern for, and emphasis on "people"---the "common" people and their messages---as prime instruments in communicating with others.

Writing in the London *News Chronicle* in 1941, Murrow explained how he went about his job: "The official news is perhaps less important than the more intimate stories of life, work, and sacrifice in Europe today," he said. The report of a night with London's fire fighters, or a day at an advance airport in Kent "while the the battle of Dunkirk was on, brings the war much nearer to the wheat farmer in Kansas than any official communique." He felt that through "human interest," involving people, he could best explain a story:

I remember seeing those unbeaten men coming back from Dunkirk; the remnants of one platoon had brought with them a quivering, shell-shocked Belgian mongrel dog. I tried to describe, that night, the dog and the men who had brought him back. Of course the fact that a dog had come to England wasn't news, but it seemed to me the best way of pointing out, of making real to people who hadn't seen it, the scenes at Dover and Folkestone.[1]

A year later, another London paper reprinted the recap of a Murrow broadcast. Headlining the story "Man-in-Street is Anglo-U.S. Hope After the War," the *Daily Sketch* thought it important to note that Murrow had said that it was time that the "common" man relate to his counterpart in the other country. Murrow also had noted that while diplomats and propagandists, officials and experts had been traded back and forth across the Atlantic, the exchange program should be expanded, in his opinion, so that American workers could go to England, and English workers to America.

He wasn't averse to sending over "not-so-common" men as well; the principle of exchanging people of all types, backgrounds, and employment was an important part of his thinking in the communication process. During the latter part of the war on a "Freedom's Forum" broadcast on education to help prepare the citizen for his postwar task, Murrow said, "I should like to see . . . a Lend-Lease Act that applied to professors, in order that we might exchange between my own country and Britain, more professors." Referring to his distinguished colleagues on the program, Harold Laski and George Malcolm Young, Murrow said, "For my part at least, I would be willing to trade several squadrons of aircraft, a few hundred tanks, if we might have Laski and Young in the States for a few years after this is over." This ideas was to come to fruition in the postwar period when the United States Congress passed the Fulbright Act of 1946 providing for a massive exchange program.

On a Sunday broadcast on the BBC's Home Service presented about the same time as his Freedom Forum program, he described the feelings that Americans had for the English and vice versa. There is mutual distrust, Murrow said, between the two countries. The English think that Americans talk big and do little. "We [Americans] think (at least some of us) that you [British] are a wearier and a wiser mother-in-law, but suspect you of condescension," Murrow noted. He pointed to the exchange that occurs among diplomats and officials who travel between the two countries, as a means of overcoming some of the common misunderstandings, but he had what he felt was a better solution:

> I wonder what would happen if you should decide to send a couple of hundred first-class British technicians to the States; men who are working here on American machines,

---

[1] *News Chronicle* (London), February 26, 1941, p. 4.

send them over not to make lectures, or to ride in parades, but to work alongside Americans, and then to bring back to this country each an American workman with him. The results might astound those who deal with communiques and mimeograph machines.

Very early in the blitz, Murrow had observed the effects of the bombing on a working-class district. Again, he talked in terms of "common" people:

> It's about the people I'd like to talk, the little people who live in those little houses, who have no uniforms and get no decoration for bravery. Those men whose only uniform was a tin hat were digging unexploded bombs out of the ground this afternoon. There were two women who gossiped across the narrow strip of tired brown grass that separated their two houses. They didn't have to open their kitchen windows in order to converse. The glass had been blown out.
>
> Those people were always calm and courageous. About an hour after the "all-clear" had sounded, people were sitting in deck chairs on their lawns, reading the Sunday papers. The girls in light, cheap dresses were strolling along the streets. There was no bravado, no loud voices, only a quiet acceptance of the situation. To me those people were incredibly brave and calm. They are the unknown heroes of this war.

On one of these wartime broadcasts, Murrow stressed the importance this concept of the "common man" had for him. It was no small part of his thinking. Averred Murrow: "The common man, or if you prefer, the common people, is no idle phrase. In my country, three times within a hundred years, there has appeared the possibility that we might achieve a new level of equality, security and individual happiness." The first occasion was under Lincoln in the Civil War, the second with Wilson at the end of World War I, and the third was the awful present of World War II. Murrow saw one reason why the first two occasions had failed. After the First World War, the understanding of the issues involved was not sufficiently widespread. "I think part of our failure was due to the fact that we did not then have a workable system of communication." Had Wilson had access to the microphone, Murrow speculated, "He would have been able to explain to the common man his stake in the world which was then being shaped."

On his brief trip home in December, 1941, he again explained his belief that the issues could best be clarified through and by the experiences of the "common" people. At a testimonial dinner given in his honor, Murrow said that he had tried to convey the "hard news of communiques and official statements," but that he had also tried to report the climate in which the news flourished:

A night with firemen . . . a morning with a demolition squad
. . . dinner with half a dozen cab drivers in a little
shelter . . . things like that may be more important than
the morning communique announcing the destruction of a dozen
aircraft.

Why was this the case? He gave a significant reason: "Evidence that the little people of Britain were losing their curious sense of humor, their fondness for grumbling at the government, their arrogant but well-mannered pride, would be much more important than news of a battle won or lost."

This emphasis on the common man, and how to reach him, was part of the central philosophy of Ed Murrow throughout his life, and a key part of his approach to communication. Eric Sevareid once commented on how angry Murrow was at him when he had written a column in the early 1960s about Latin America, making a statement to the effect that there was no such thing as world opinion---it was an abstraction that had no meaning in a moralistic sense. Murrow told him, "I'm sorry to see you abandon your principles so easily." Sevareid said later that he should have replied to this criticism with the point that it was not principles, but strategies he had been talking about. Sevareid added:

> He had this faith that somehow the power of words, persuasion, even among enemy countries, or enemy ideologies, this 'winning the hearts and minds of people' idea . . . . He really seemed to believe that . . . . And by that time, I'd come down to the deepest doubts about all this. This was a much tougher game than that. People wanted to be on the winning side, not necessarily on the righteous side, in many situations.
>
> I'd been in Asia and Africa and quite a few places, and I was getting rather jaundiced about a lot of these assumptions we made. And this upset Ed. But I think I was basically right about it.
>
> He was a great idealist, you know.
>
> The power of words among like-minded people, or similar cultures, traditions, like Britain and America . . . is *one* thing, but the idea that between very alien peoples, we get to know each other well, going to have peace, and solve these things, like each other, the Eisenhower people-to-people thing, I think Ed probably believed in all that.
>
> I came really not to believe it very much. People respond to power situations.

In talking across the ocean, Murrow expressed his belief that the communication process had to be "open" and "honest." And that problem could only be solved through meeting issues head-on and speaking directly, not only to the issue, but to each other. There was a need for more "frank talk," and there had to be the courage not to shy away from controversy. Throughout the wartime period, Murrow referred again and again to these beliefs. In 1942 he said, "If this war is to be anything other than a prelude to the third world war we must begin to use our common language and say to each other just what we mean."

On a BBC broadcast the year before, he interviewed historian Allan Nevins about American aid to Britain. Twice during that interview, Murrow said that "there seems to be very little frank talk across the Atlantic about this lending of a garden hose" in a reference to the Lend-Lease idea. Then he said that it was his "personal opinion" that American public opinion, which would have a great effect on the speed of production in American shipyards, "might become more concerned about this whole problem of ships and shipping if a little more frank talk on the subject passed back and forth across the Atlantic."

After he had made a visit back to the United States in late 1941, Murrow proceeded to tell the British what questions Americans were asking about England, and how American thinking about the war had changed. In a BBC broadcast he said:

> There are more serious and perhaps sinister questions being asked about Britain. I see no reason why they should not be discussed frankly and openly across the Atlantic. Indeed, we might understand each other better if we had more frank conversations between Britons and Americans.

It was a fascinating broadcast, for as a good polemicist on an issue, as a former debater, Murrow sought to encourage a bond of common ground before he went into the critical questions that he found his countrymen to be asking. The "communicator" laid out his premises:

> First you must bear in mind that we [the American people] are, on the whole, more emotional, vociferous and intolerant than you. We'll go to a baseball game or a football match and shout for the blood of the referee, and, on occasions, fling beer bottles at him. Our domestic controversies are conducted in strong language, with much name-calling---in short, we're inclined to say what we think even when we have not thought very much.

Believing that "honest and frank talk" had at no time cost him a friend in Britain, he launched into a criticism of Britain. Why were three and a half million soldiers kept in England? Why couldn't the RAF knock out big guns across the channel? He also tried to explain that such questions came out of a perspective that could be vastly different in a large land thirty-five hundred miles away than from a small island.

In 1943, Murrow reported in a CBS broadcast home that it had been a source of satisfaction during his years in Britain to see that Anglo-American relations were growing stronger every year, and he stressed again: "Another force for good in promoting international relations is fair, honest news from over here, accurately reported there at home. Frankness and honesty *may* divide America and Britain, but polite fiction *certainly* will." This statement gets to the very heart of Edward R. Murrow's broadcast philosophy.

It is well known that Murrow was not reluctant to grapple with controversy. His attitudes on controversy were evident early in his career. In fact, he felt that it was a method of attracting listeners, an idea that sponsors or networks have not exactly adopted. From Murrow's perspective: "Whenever broadcasting can stand in the centre of a controversy, giving both sides an equal opportunity to present their claims, the number of listeners is likely to increase."

But controversy was important to Murrow for reasons other than attracting audiences. It was indispensable for getting results. In a discussion of Britain's plans for reconstruction on the "Freedom Forum" series, Murrow noted that the government was a coalition government, a government in which controversy was supposed to be ruled out. But the reconstruction plans being considered would certainly lead to controversial legislation. "How are you going to get change without controversy?" he queried.

One statement Murrow made during the war reveals that he did not adopt the term "journalism" as the word describing what he did. While the broader definition is used today to describe the work of the reporter in a variety of media, he used it in its narrower sense---of one who records "in a journal": thus, the print reporter. Commenting on the pressures of time, he said, "At times like that I almost envy the American journalists who are reporting from London."

On the program "The World Goes By," series host F. H. Grisewood urged Murrow and Fred Bate of NBC to spell out the differences between what the "journalists" did and what they did. Both agreed that there was confusion in many people's minds about the differences between broadcasting and the press. Bate thought the two media were "fundamentally complementary" as they applied to news. Murrow responded, "That's right. For example, it's very difficult, if not impossible, for a broadcaster from London to discuss in detail a new budget---people just won't listen. That can be done in print. But broadcasting can describe the scene in the House of Commons, the atmosphere, and the comments of the man in the street in a way that print can't touch." He also added that material is broadcast that you wouldn't think of cabling for print. "The little human interest stories which mean so much if you hear them" wouldn't come alive otherwise, in print.

On that "World Goes By" program, the two men analyzed the advantages and disadvantages involved in being their own final editors as follows:

> Ed: There's one big advantage we have, and that is that no one in New York can rewrite or change our material. We say what we see and no one can insert lurid adjectives or qualifying phrases.
> Fred: Yes, and that's a two-edged advantage. As you said, a word once spoken . . . is gone . . . beyond recall.
> Ed: And sometimes, how we'd like to call it back. Yes! I remember once talking from Wimbledon, trying to fill in time during a short shower when play on the centre court had stopped. I did a glowing description of Sir Samuel Hoare arriving with the Duchess of Kent and asserted firmly

that Sir Samuel was wearing a saucy black straw hat with white ribbon trailing down his back.

Even the senses can deceive the professional eyewitness observer. In recalling one episode, Fred Bate cited the time he and Ed covered the "bombing" of the Portsmouth Navy Yard. They saw black smoke, a huge cloud. But the Navy Yard was intact. Smoke from a burning building on a hill beyond had rolled down over the Admiralty property. Murrow cautioned: "That stands out as proving that you can't believe everything you think you see."

Pointing to the limits of radio and print, Murrow told of one of his most memorable reporting episodes:

> Remember the day when we were just outside an airdrome when it was bombed? Remember the nice smell of that grass as we lay in the ditch? The all-clear then sounded, and they were standing outside the entrance to the airdrome. At that moment, a company of young ladies in RAF blue marched through the gates into that battered airdrome. Their chins were up; some of them wore a little too much makeup; some of them, I am sure, were afraid; but they were steady and smiling. That's the sort of story that's hard to tell either in print or on the air.

Perhaps even television could not tell that story. With the most sophisticated media available, it is still difficult to communicate the all-important inner life of a story to an audience.

More threads of belief about reporting can be gathered from other comments Murrow made. One important conviction was the "criticism" of British policy had to be reported. If it were news, such criticism could not be whitewashed. "We have been concerned to hold a mirror behind Britain at war, striving to reflect a true picture by means of the spoken word." And when the leaders or the British press had criticized government policy, "that criticism has often been heard in Vancouver, British Columbia, before the newspapers containing it reached the streets of London." Most reporters were telling the story as honestly as they could, Murrow maintained, "if for no other reason than that they may live in peace with their own conscience." His ideal was clearly in the tradition of a libertarian philosophy of communications:

> We have recorded British victories and defeat, criticisms of Cabinet Ministers, believing always that the intrusion of personal prejudice and prophecy is useless, if not harmful, and that the listener in America, if given sufficient information, will make up his mind in accordance with the ultimate truth.

This was only good sense, Murrow thought, for you couldn't fool the audience anyway. "Certainly the listeners are more alive to prejudicial and tendentious reporting than they were." He added that there was a practice of giving critics time on the air in which to criticize reporters, a practice "that's effective and increases listeners."

What about the reporter's subjectivity intruding? (Or is this being "involved" and perhaps more accurately conveying the nuances of feeling and action in a story?) When asked to what extent the American commentators analyze news and interpret it, he responded,

> Too much, I think. The broadcasts we do from Europe might be called straight reporting, but some American commentators [and inserted in this BBC script in pencil are the words 'those that sit in air-conditioned studios in New York,' implying a detached and somewhat soft environment] engage in a great deal of interpretive, if not editorial broadcasting.

He added that this isn't as bad as it might sound, since there are three national networks, and if the listener objects to the tone of one commentator, he can listen to another.

These remarks do not mean that Murrow was not a commentator in these early days, or that "objectivity" was his total aim in reporting. "An individual who can entirely avoid being influenced by the atmosphere in which he works might not even be a good reporter," he said on another occasion. He stated in the same context, however, that in reporting the war, he had tried to prevent his own prejudices and loyalties from "coming between you and the information which it was our duty to impart." Furthermore, he felt, "It is no part of a reporter's function to advocate policy. The most I can do is to indicate certain questions facing America . . . you must supply the answers."

Still, there came a time for Murrow when:

> Occasionally, in reporting this war, the reporter is obliged to express his personal opinion, his own evaluation of the mass of confusing and contradictory statements, communiques, speeches by statesmen, and personal interviews.
>
> It has always seemed to me that such statements of personal opinion should be frankly labeled as such without any attempt to cloak one's own impressions or opinions in an aura of omnipotence.
>
> What I think of events in Europe is no more important than what you think, but I do have certain opportunities for observation and study.

These reflections from various writings and broadcasts of Ed Murrow reveal that he understood that the reporting process was a rather complicated one. He understood instinctively that pure and total objectivity was a quality that even the professional observer and interpreter of events could not always attain---nor for that matter was it necessarily desirable. Still, the need to bring out all issues and significant angles of a problem was paramount, and if comment were inserted (and it had to be so labeled if it were), an honest and open attempt to tell the story as best the reporter could was the all-important goal.

These are essential parts of the philosophy of reporting held by the man who organized the overseas CBS news staff in the 1930s and who hired many of the men of whom some, in the 1970s, are still reporting daily to the American public. One of these men---Eric Sevareid---wrote some years ago on the same subject in his challenging book, *Not So Wild a Dream*: "Every journalist, since time and space are limited, must select the facts he will present, the quotations he will emphasize. He is not a machine, and he does not work in a vacuum."

While obviously there were many influences on Murrow's thinking, certainly an important way of testing and evolving his ideas was in his discussions with other significant leaders. On two such occasions, Murrow wrestled with questions relating to the role of the press and the nature of broadcast systems.

In the summer of 1942, Murrow became involved in another challenging analysis on the role of the press on one of the BBC's "Freedom Forum" programs. Sir Frederick Whyte, KCSI, was the moderator, and the panelists were George Malcolm Young, Murrow, and Harold Laski. The program opened with a discussion of "security censorship," which Murrow defined as a control only over information that might be of some value to an enemy. He emphasized his idea that editors and reporters were entirely free to say whatever they liked about government policy.

Throughout the program, principles and practices of journalism were analyzed, with most of the comments coming from Laski and Young, with Murrow presumably listening. On selectivity Young said, "As soon as you make any selection, you're beginning to influence the mind of the reader." Even the style of writing and the placement of the story in the paper affect the reader.

Young deplored the emphasis on "entertainment" that had crept into papers in the twentieth century. Papers decided that readers wanted to be amused rather than informed. As a result, news became what the editor thought was interesting or entertaining. Young felt that readers had to be educated. To pick up the conversation from there, Murrow suggested that perhaps others needed educating as well:

    Ed: Education of the readers and education of the editors as well?
    Young: Education of editors is a different thing---an education in responsibility.
    Ed: But not compulsion?
    Young: No.

Then the issue of controls entered the discussion. Murrow asked about postwar controls on the press. Laski emphatically decried any government dictation to the news media. It would be an "outrage on human decency." On the other hand, he didn't want the paper to be free to say what it pleased, "irrelevantly to all the facts that it encounters." There had to be some method, he felt, by which a framework of reasonable truthfulness could underlie the work of the press.

"What methods?" Murrow asked. Several ideas were tossed out. One suggested that if an editor lied about government, he should be compelled to print a contradiction of the lie equal in space and location. This point was made, interestingly, more than two decades before "access" to print media and a "fairness doctrine" for print media came into public debate in the United States. A diversity of papers appealing to different educational levels of audiences was also suggested. All agreed that separate news columns divorced from opinion were imperative.

Murrow set down another condition, that there would be no rewrite men, particularly rewriting the material sent in by his foreign correspondents:

> Laski: Absolutely.
> Ed: I would find good men, and send them to Budapest or wherever it happened to be, and then their material would be published as written, and it would not be suppressed or whole paragraphs deleted, as was the case in both countries with some of the dispatches that came out of Middle Europe before the war.

On another occasion, very early in the war, Murrow revealed his philosophy of broadcasting, its power, and how it functioned in a commercial context. This exposition offerred an illuminating look at his early attitude toward commercial broadcasting, a position that was in some contrast to the more pessimistic view he held later in his career.

This analysis occurred while he was discussing broadcasting with colleagues Colin Wills of Australia and R. J. Montgomery of South Africa on a BBC program entitled, "Meet Uncle Sam." During the course of the program, Wills asked Murrow how important entertainment was on American radio. Ed conceded that most time is devoted to entertainment on radio: "The objective is always to lure listeners away from the competing radio networks." Montgomery agreed that this approach would tend to put the entertainment value of programs first and their educational value second:

> Montgomery: If most want jazz over symphony, would you limit the second for the sake of business?
> Ed: Yes. American broadcasting operates on the assumption that it must give the public what it wants. With very few exceptions broadcasters don't believe that they are intelligent enough [and here the script "to give the American public what is good for it" is lined out with pencil. And in the place of this lined-out phrase is written the following, in pencil] to decide what's good for the public.

An interesting piece of editing. Wills pressed on. "But don't you think sometimes the public gets to like what it's given?" Murrow evaded, with humor and good will: "It's a good thing for us. Otherwise we might be out of a job."

How did Murrow see "competition" working on radio? He continued in a more serious manner. "If you have jazz music on one network, you are likely to find symphonic music on another. You may have the Metropolitan Opera and Charlie McCarthy being broadcast at the same time on two different networks. You can take your choice."

But certainly, Wills felt, the emphasis on majority tastes would tend to push out important minority issues. Murrow tossed the ball back, asking how the matter was handled in Australia. Wills responded that a public corporation like the BBC was an agency which "gives the public what some people think is good for it." In competition are hundreds of commercial stations offering largely entertainment programs that are "wanted" by the public.

Murrow bristled when Montgomery described the South African broadcasting system as one in which the listener is saved "from the somewhat sickening announcements [of commercial broadcasting stations] like telling you to keep your teeth clean, in the middle of a symphony concert." Murrow answered that the more objectionable advertising was off the air and had been for some time. And even if at times it might be offensive to be told in a "confidential, pleading tone that I must use a certain hair tonic to keep my charm, . . . I would prefer that to having a few bureaucrats in Washington deciding what I can or cannot hear."

Later in the broadcast, after defending the commercial aspects of the system, Murrow clearly emphasized his own interest in the medium:

> But the thing that interests me about broadcasting is its *ability to inform the listener and to determine his action* [italics added]. It's always worth remembering that in all three of Mr. Roosevelt's presidential campaigns he had more than 80 per cent of the press against him. A year ago, his whole presidential campaign consisted of five radio broadcasts made in the weeks preceding the election.

Montgomery concluded the program with a question to Murrow that has extreme relevance in our time. With the power over public opinion which he had just demonstrated in his reference to FDR's campaigns, to what extent could American radio sway public opinion "if the U.S.A. should suddenly be faced by a very grave decision, such as entering this war"?

Murrow's first thoughts were on the fairness with which radio was handling the issue. At the time, he felt, the country was not united on this question, but "when the decision is reached, broadcasting will have been a determining factor." One of the leading opponents of American involvement in the war, Charles Lindbergh, got his say on the air; arguments about entering the war or not were "fought out in an incredible number of broadcasts for and against." He concluded: "Radio has 'sold' many things in America and it may be used yet to 'sell' the nation on the idea that the time has come when Americans must look their obligations and their enemies squarely in the eye."

On still another "Freedom Forum" program, Murrow more succinctly---and somewhat more eloquently and positively---spelled out his attitudes on American broadcasting: "If one compares American and British broadcasting, you get really a comparison of Britain and the United States." In America, "our system is commercial, it's fast, sometimes it's noisy, it's technically slick, very controversial and on the whole very free." As for Britain, as Murrow saw it, "British broadcasting is more conservative, cautious, sometimes perhaps has even a little higher regard for fact than we have." In a superbly pointed conclusion appended to the statement that reflected his political astuteness, Harold Laski added, "When you know who are the controllers, and what they're controlling it for, you know what the real purpose of the wireless system or the press system of any country is."

The problem, then as now, was the knowledge, clearly admitted, that there are unavoidable controls of one kind or another on the major mass media. After all, someone has to make decisions, someone edits the news copy. "How does one get a reliable body of controllers?" it was asked. Murrow answered, "Why isn't it possible that so far as broadcasting is concerned, the listener should have something to say about it? And certainly under a competitive system, the one that attracts the greatest number of listeners is likely to be exercising the best judgment." Translated, this statement lends strong support to the long-standing industry argument in the United States about programming: "We give the public what it wants."

Murrow subsequently was asked: "In the United States, control is really supplied by the consumer?" He answered, "Yes, very likely, under a competitive system." "Very likely" seems an unsure rejoinder. Would the solution be to have stations that just specialized in one kind of broadcasting? Or several stations offering their own complete service? Murrow felt certain of one thing:

> If the programmes are not satisfactory . . . it soon becomes quite clear that the listeners are transferring their allegiance to another network, or station. . . . [and] It's no good putting on broadcasts unless they're listened to.

Perhaps the point has been somewhat labored here, but it is important to establish what Murrow felt about his medium and its handling of news, and what journalism and the press actually meant to him. He believed in the power of radio, knowing how great was its power to influence. But he also recognized the complexity of the role of reporter and the necessity for responsible dedication in carrying out the task.

It is also clear that Murrow, during his years in England, seemed to feel that responsible journalism, as he saw it, was not incompatible with a commercial system of broadcasting. When pressed, it seemed he was quite able---and willing---to defend the American system of broadcasting. Time and experience---and perhaps reflection on the attitudes expressed by such men as Laski, Young, and his BBC colleagues---modified and embittered him. For, two decades later, he publicly expressed what he felt were grave, if not indeed fatal, failures in the commercial system. "Giving the public what it wanted" for Murrow became increasingly a case for developing the media into a vast wasteland of mediocrity.

How did others perceive Murrow's understanding of his medium and his work? Michael Standing put it this way: "His great preoccupation was with people. Not with conventions or trappings of behavior, he was really concerned with the effects on the future of people." And what was the medium for? How would it be used? Certainly with "selectivity" by the public, thought Standing. While there were arguments for exposing all facets of opinion on any and every issue, he felt that Murrow was a person who would not want to "open the microphone utterly, widely, without careful thought. He would have seen the grave dangers in that. Many arguments and views and philosophies are superficially persuasive and if not deeply assimilated and carefully thought out can do a great deal more harm than good." While this view of Murrow's thinking on media seems to reflect a qualified---albeit ethically based---restriction on the role of opinion on the air, Standing reiterated what others have strongly felt:

> I think he always was concerned with---this I do know---with communication between the general level of people as opposed to the articulate and upper strata, and political beings. He was much more concerned with the communication of "people-to-people," as he used to call his program. This was the level of ordinary people, wanting to talk and meet and oppose views or align views.

Leonard Miall felt that Murrow was very interested in the technicalities of the thing with which he was working. He always wanted to know what the microphone could do, what the television camera was able to portray, and how.

Charles Collingwood, whose day-to-day life in London often dovetailed with Murrow's, is perhaps one of those best qualified to provide an interpretation of Ed Murrow's philosophy of communications. He worked with Murrow in London until the end of the war.

Recalling when he first went to work for Murrow, Collingwood said that he expected to spend some time learning the new trade. He went over some of Murrow's scripts with great care, and on the second day or so that he was on the job, Collingwood told Murrow that he noticed that he used very short sentences, usually declarative in structure. He asked Murrow if that was the secret of the technique of broadcast journalism. Ed replied, "Do I use short sentences like this? I never really thought about it."

Collingwood, when later queried about Murrow's reply, added "I don't suppose he ever did. He broadcast in what was his natural style. And that was one of the first things he taught me, early in the game."

One day, Murrow said that he had a dinner date and asked Collingwood to do the broadcast. Collingwood described the situation that resulted:

> I got in there early. I went through everything. No sign of Ed. I'd been with him when he did them, and I knew how to get into the BBC, the bowels of it from which we broadcast.
> Ten minutes before the broadcast, I gave a copy of the script to the censor and got it back and I wasn't sure what was going to happen.
> A couple of minutes, honestly no more than that, Ed sort of slid into the seat opposite me, and we talked to New York. And they said, "Now, to Charles Collingwood in London." First time on the air and I launched into my broadcast. But I hadn't remembered that you had to sign off. I think in those days we said, "Now, back to Bob Trout [or whoever it was] in New York."
> And I finished my broadcast and stopped. Ed casually leaned forward into the mike, and said, "Now, back to Bob Trout in New York." I was anxious for a critique of the broadcast and he said, "Oh, it was fine, everything was fine."
> Next day, he asked me to do the broadcast again. I kept asking for a critique, but it wasn't for about ten days. Ed finally said, "you don't have to speak so loud. These microphones are very good. You sound a little bit as though you're talking on a long-distance telephone.

But Collingwood wanted more than just this, and he kept prodding his employer for more comments and suggestions. Murrow finally said, "The important thing is that you be yourself, and speak and broadcast in your own way. The last thing I want you to do is sound like me." Summing up this episode, Collingwood smiled and added, "Ed was a remarkable psychologist."

Years later, Collingwood was asked what Murrow expected of his employees. What did he want in a newsman? What did he want you to do? What did he see in a person? Collingwood answered: "What he saw in me, I couldn't possibly tell you, because I was a very brash young man. What he continually laid emphasis on was accuracy and impartiality." He added that Ed was never a preacher, although some thought he had that reputation. Collingwood continued:

> He never felt it was part of a broadcaster's duty, or indeed, any part of his business, to persuade, although heaven knows his broadcasts from London were very persuasive. His deep commitment to the British people, and to the allied cause, came through very clearly, but he never did it in a sermonizing way.

Collingwood, in analyzing Murrow's style, also stressed that Murrow expected his people to broadcast the "significant detail" of a story. For Murrow, this meant: "Find the significant detail which gives color to a radio broadcast where there are no pictures; it helps to create the picture in the mind of the listener." Murrow was thus acutely aware of that quality of radio which, aside from some FM programming and specialty stations, has largely been abandoned. Radio's "imaginative" quality, its ability to create a picture of a scene in the minds of its listeners as would a storyteller, was a quality Murrow used well and saw as a distinct attribute and asset of the medium.

Collingwood observed that there was, of course, much ado about the quality of voice in the heyday of radio reporting, but that "Ed certainly wasn't interested in the quality of voice, which was much exaggerated." He wanted reporters who were understandable, of course, but he didn't care about great resonance. He did want a correspondent to be something more than "just a good reporter." But what did he really want in his staff in a positive sense? What does it mean to be "more than 'just a good reporter'"? Collingwood observed that there was "obviously a common denominator, because a group came to be known within CBS as 'Murrow's boys,' or 'Murrow's team.'" When confronted about specifics needed for an answer, Collingwood, after a brief pause and some thinking out loud, said with what one could only describe as thoughtful enthusiasm, "I think he rather wanted, or at least admired, in correspondents a certain quality of reflectiveness, of being able to get beneath the surface of events."

What about training for the profession? "Ed always used to maintain," Collingwood said, "that the technical side of journalism could be learned by anyone reasonably intelligent in a few months; it was the practice of it which counted. I've always felt that way myself."

While Miall said that Murrow was alive to the instruments of the trade, was aware of how they could be used and what they could do, Collingwood clearly emphasized that this did not mean he was a technical wizard. Not by a long shot. Noted Collingwood: "Ed never could understand how a tape recorder would work, or a broadcast; it was all magic to him. Later in television the intricate details of communication were all a great mystery to him."

Years later, Charles Collingwood was asked to summarize, if he could, Murrow's philosophy of broadcasting. How did Murrow perceive the role of the new electronic media? Collingwood summarized well. First of all, Murrow understood the enormous importance of electronic journalism as a factor in public opinion, in making up people's minds about what was happening in the world, in convincing them to act, and in influencing their course of action. People had to be informed. Therefore, these most informative media had to be treated seriously. ("He was essentially an unfrivolous man, anyway.") Time could not be wasted. In doing the evening newscasts, Murrow tried to get all of the important stories into the broadcast that he could, knowing full well that they might not be the "flashiest or the most attention-getting." He knew of the great problem that the shortness of time imposed on the media, as Collingwood noted:

He struggled until the end of his life in connection with broadcasting, struggled to find a proper way to use this time to inform people while at the same time knowing there was never time enough to tell them everything they ought to know.

Ed struggled with this problem as hard as he could. It was one of the reasons why he became such a great documentarian, in both radio and television. The idea that sometime we must take a long look at some key subject which cannot be covered in the thirty seconds you've got.

Although the problems have grown worse with each passing year, according to Collingwood, Murrow was well aware of most of them already during the war years. Some problems, or issues, were not so easily handled, however, such as the basic one that poses the question of commercial versus public broadcasting. That issue was critical in that soul-reaching and eloquent speech delivered by Murrow in 1958 to the Radio-Television News Directors Association in Chicago. Was this the final statement of a totally disillusioned man who had solved most of the problems that had confronted him but seemed trapped by this key issue? Had he really changed his thinking to the extent that he not only no longer praised commercial broadcasting but regarded it as a bane on his profession?

Collingwood answered: "I think he realized the structural nature of the problem. It is built in. Here you have a medium which is not fundamentally, as a newspaper is, a news-disseminating medium." This is a particularly critical problem when polls continually reveal that most people get most of their view of the world from television. The frustration comes because television is the greatest news-disseminating medium devised by man. Yet, "it is fundamentally an entertainment medium. In a newspaper, the crossword puzzle and the comic strips are secondary. In television they're primary, and the news is secondary."

Collingwood elaborated:

How to reconcile the responsibilities of broadcasting as an informative medium---with its responsibilities to make a profit, which you have to do if you're to stay in business as an entertainment medium---was a continual perplexity to him.

He came down quite clearly, as I suppose all news broadcasters do, on the side of more time, which is space in our business, more time for news.

It was a problem he was not able to resolve, which has not been resolved yet, and---I don't know---won't be until modern technology makes it possible to have, to broadcast under a different structural arrangement than now exists.

The essential theory of communications and broadcasting, their role, and the role of the journalist in the electronic media---these were the ideas that concerned Ed Murrow as he embarked on the day-to-day practice of his profession. But as Collingwood said, it was the "practice" that counted, not the theory.

Murrow in time came to realize that, while commercial broadcasting was essential in the American scheme of things, its impact and operations, based on popular choice, would not produce the best of all possible broadcasting worlds. As Alexis de Tocqueville had noted over a century earlier, American democracy with all its vitality and progress yet was fraught with the danger that the demands of the masses of people might instill standards of mediocrity. These mass standards could, in the contemporary world, limit the great potential of the new mass media of communication--radio and television.

CHAPTER VII

REPORTING: RADIO, TV, AND INTERVIEWING--

SOME SPECIFICS

In exploring what Edward R. Murrow had to say about the daily practice of his profession, some enlightening clues emerge that help to describe his basic nature and philosophy of broadcast journalism. Ed Murrow did not harbor the rapport for the written word that he obviously had for the spoken, with the result that many of his ideas, views, and practices have remained obscure. While he wrote a few articles during the wartime years, they seemed indirectly (and a few, directly) apologetic in tone about the difficulty of laying out words in cold, dark print. He left his scripts, but no major book or novel. He said it best himself in an article in 1941: "To a broadcaster there is something rather frightening about being asked to write for print. It's such a cold, impersonal and permanent medium. I never read anything of my own in print without a rather hot, embarrassed feeling."

A most revealing statement on the evolving roles of radio and television and interviewing technique was made by Ed Murrow on television in England during the 1950s when he was the guest of Malcolm Muggeridge on "Panorama," the show founded by Richard Dimbleby. In that presentation, Murrow's personal values and concepts of the media came ringing through. He seemed to be in a relaxed and comfortable mood. With the ever-present cigarette throughout, he alternately bantered with Muggeridge, became serious, even threw his head back with a loud laugh at one point. Perhaps the reversal of roles relaxed him; he was not often cast as interviewee. He was at that time at the height of his popularity in the United States, since the program was broadcast just a year after his famous McCarthy expose.

Muggeridge initiated the interview by asking Murrow how he could interview people so interestingly and say so little. Murrow replied that the process of interviewing "consists in finding an interesting person, and then finding questions to ask him." And what happens, Muggeridge continued, if the person were not interesting? Murrow's reply: "You listen harder than you do normally. [You] Concentrate on the person's hobbies and off-beat interests." As for interviewing on television, Murrow added: "I prefer doing an interview with the camera working over my shoulder, so that the interviewer does not get between the subject and the audience, so that the subject in fact is talking to the audience and not to me."

Murrow said that he never knew exactly where he was going in an interview, that his questions came from the preceding answers. "I'm very much opposed to a rehearsed, planned interview," he insisted. However, to digress a moment, according to

Mary Adams, Murrow would "play the game" if required. Mary Adams was in charge of talks and documentaries in the BBC television service after the war, and she had earlier arranged scientific talks for the BBC. According to Mary Adams: "One day he [Murrow] was going to participate in a discussion program, but missed the rehearsal." At the time, Adams explained, all conversations were typed up from shorthand for rehearsal and later reading. Ed arrived just moments before air time and was rather unhappy with the prepared script. "Well, guess I will have to go along. Not much I can do now," he reportedly said. "He played the game," Adams emphasized.

To return to the "Panorama" program, Murrow told Muggeridge that, in his opinion, the reason his interview with Dr. Robert Oppenheimer was so fascinating was because he didn't know enough about the subject of high energy physics and the development of the atomic bomb to ask specific questions. "I didn't, in effect, know what he was talking about," confessed Murrow.

Leonard Miall once asked Murrow for advice on interviewing people. According to Miall, "One of his pieces of advice was not to ask a question. If you just simply keep quiet, the man you're interviewing feels an obligation to go on and say something."

To the end of his career, Edward R. Murrow, who gained national recognition from his television appearances in the United States, never seemed to develop a warm, personal rapport with the visual medium. He related, rather, to sound, words, radio. He always expressed this relationship positively; with television he always seemed to feel uncomfortable, incomplete. He was worried about what it could do. These matters were much under discussion in the interview with Muggeridge on "Panorama." " I don't think TV has taken the place of sound broadcasting so far as news is concerned," Murrow stated. "In the field of news it is basically a pictorial supplement, where you have a set spectacle, a coronation." With such an event, explained Murrow, no medium can match the presentation. But, he stressed, "News consists to a large extent of ideas. You know how difficult it is to translate ideas into words. But then, when you have to translate them into pictures as well, it becomes exceedingly difficult." As Murrow saw it, television was just an added code that had to be translated: idea to words to picture.

Murrow continued to be optimistic about the role of radio: "I don't believe that television is going to replace radio." Muggeridge said that television coverage of the American political conventions seemed so complete. To the extent that it was a "set, predictable spectacle," Murrow agreed. "But when it came to finding out what was happening in the party caucus . . . the old reportorial effort had still to be applied," he noted.

Radio, Murrow was convinced, would survive television, and there would be a different type of news reporting on this medium. "It will go into greater depth," he said. Its role, its new job would be to supply what was needed behind the news, so it could be understood: "Radio will have to devote more time to backgrounding the news, not only saying this happened, but this is the background, this is what caused it to happen, and these are the results and the consequences that may be expected to flow from it." In the main, from the contemporary perspective, it would seem that Murrow's hope for the future role of radio has not been realized, and television has devoted only a tiny portion of its time to "backgrounding," explaining and probing the news. And we might conclude from these facts that this lack of intelligent news analysis constitutes a major problem of the mass media of communication today.

Murrow's feeling for radio may best be demonstrated by his own regard for one particular award. He once told Malcolm Muggeridge precisely what he prized most in his---by then---many years of public and private recognition:

> This is the only trophy I have ever kept and I have received many. . . . the most touching thing that ever happened to me. When I left here after nine years, they went down and just cut loose that old-fashioned microphone, literally cut the cable, put a little plaque on it, which said in substance, This is from Studio B-4, for Murrow who used it, [and] I think they said, with some distinction. . . This I value above anything I have.

Perhaps the best explanation for Murrow's feelings about radio are provided in his famous comment about his role in covering Britain during the war years. Earlier in the program, Murrow had told Muggeridge how good it felt to be back in London, "where I left all of my youth, and much of my heart." Twice, on the air, he made that comment that day.

More than a cognitive awareness of the role that radio could play in contrast to other modern media, there was in Murrow's heart an affectionate personal regard for a symbol, a special symbol, of the *sound* medium.

"What about television?" Muggeridge wanted to know. What could commercial television mean to Britain? This kinescope film then gave perhaps the only glimpse ever of Ed Murrow throwing his head back with a spontaneous and hearty laugh. Quickly he reassumed that rather long and serious look, puffed on his cigarette, and replied in deep tones that he had "learned when the British go abroad, they don't counsel others." To discuss the relative merits of British and American television would be an "utterly futile undertaking." Murrow continued, "If you compare the two systems . . . you come down to a comparison of the two countries." His conclusion (this was 1955) was that "neither system could be transplanted effectively to the other country." In the few remaining years he had to work in commercial television, the sense of "acceptance" that he seemed to show here in reference to a commercial system of broadcasting would certainly be somewhat modified. Or so his 1958 speech to the Radio-Television News Directors Association would seem to indicate. But more about that later.

In his crisp and descriptive style, however, Murrow did tell Muggeridge that American radio---and perhaps television---"is

highly competitive, it is commercial, it is loud, it is vulgar
. . . at times vulgar . . . it is experimental." On the other
hand,

> . . . British broadcasting is careful, cautious, rather
> paternalistic and . . .
> Muggeridge interrupting: Vulgar.
> Murrow: Not quite so vulgar so often. Both . . .
> are accurate reflections of the political, social and
> economic climate in which the two grew up.

Finally, as the interview was concluding, both men avowed that they favored "competition" in the media, with Muggeridge emphasizing repeatedly his hatred of monopoly. Yet that distaste for monopoly did not produce a condemnation of the governmentally operated BBC monopoly that existed in those days.

Some years earlier, toward the end of the war, Murrow was interviewing D. H. Munro, the BBC's television production manager, on a program entitled "Television Was Fun." In the course of it, the announcer asked Murrow if he had seen any British television before the war. Murrow replied:

> Yes, I did. And the thing that impressed me the most
> was the complexity of the whole thing. . . . As I looked
> down on the studio floor it seemed to contain an army of
> people. And the pace looked terrific. To me it seemed a
> miracle that the picture on the screen was so dispassionate
> . . . and in the control room itself, there was so much
> going on. . . . You know, before the war I saw television
> in this country, in France, in Germany, and at home in the
> States, and you fellows certainly led the world when it
> came to producing programmes. How did you do it, Munro?

To Murrow's mind, television was, at least at its early stage of development, a large and cumbersome, confused and complex giant. Robert Reid recalls a visit he made to New York during the 1950s, when he watched one of the telecasts of "See It Now." On the way back from the studio to Murrow's apartment, Reid remembers, he and Murrow talked about radio and television. Murrow told him that he didn't think much of television because it was conditioned too much by the visual context, by pictures. He sensed that one could get infinitely more into radio by way of facts and information. The great danger in television for Murrow was that editors would often select a subject or an approach because there was a good picture to build it around. Important facts and events should dictate priorities, as far as Murrow was concerned, rather than television picture opportunities.

Still, Reid believed that Murrow had a complete grasp of television as well as the radio medium. When they arrived at Murrow's apartment that night, Murrow's first reaction was to confer privately with his son, Casey, about the program and to attempt to get Casey's reaction to it. The program had dealt with cancer, with the emphasis on how the morbidity of the subject was conquered in one midwestern town by holding a parade of many people who had been cured of cancer. While Murrow was willing to admit that the pictures of the parade and other events had increased interest on the part of the viewing public, he offered a more general and limited conclusion: "I'd like to get in more facts and information, but too often pictures are used because they look nice and really have no bearing . . . on what you're dealing with."

In discussing Ed Murrow's philosophy of communication and the job of a journalist, in examining his views on radio versus television, and in seeking his advice on how to conduct interviews, his goals and beliefs and directives for behavior are all related to his own practices. Collingwood once said of Murrow that he had always believed that the technical details of the job could be learned, and that practice is what really counted. And, in Collingwood's view, there was little question of Murrow's ability to practice what he preached: "He was a communicator in the most professional sense. And that of course is what the times needed, and why Ed Murrow really set the standards by which broadcast journalism measures itself today."

In reading the scripts of Murrow broadcasts, one could choose a variety of examples to illustrate the application of Murrow's theory. Certain scripts could best demonstrate one aspect or another of his philosophy. Many of his famous ones---his broadcast after Buchenwald, or the raid over Berlin---are among the literate and permanently prized pieces written in the English language.

There are a couple of broadcasts less well known, particularly to Americans since they were beamed to Britain, which illustrate his entire philosophy of communication. These scripts are overt attempts to bring understanding between peoples. For Murrow, in the last analysis, what happened on the political or social scene---a McCarthy witch hunt, a Cuban revolution, standing "steady" against Hitler---was not just a matter of persuasion or pontification, but simply a case of abstracting downward to the common people. It was above all else a matter of individual human beings and their relationships to one another. Throughout the war, in broadcast after broadcast and in one speech and article after another, he pleaded for greater understanding among people individually and peoples of different cultures. He "pleaded," that is, only in the sense that he constantly emphasized what was possible and desirable in the way of improved human relationships.

Ed Murrow would have been interested to note how today's jet age has made it possible for small armies of young people from America and other countries regularly to walk or cycle the byways of Europe. He would have recalled his own earlier, more difficult days of travel between the continents, and his pre-broadcasting trips as a student and faculty exchange coordinator. He would, undoubtedly, have found a significant hope for the world in these increasing contacts, no matter how complex and dangerous the many crises facing our modern world and how pessimistic he might have been about some of them.

In focusing on Murrow's "communication" practices, one cannot overlook how old BBC comrades and colleagues respected Murrow's style and techniques. Leonard Miall, for example, liked to recall those days when the BBC assigned him to come to the States as its first permanent news correspondent. This was shortly after the death of President Franklin Roosevelt, and Murrow was nearing the end of his tenure in Britain. "As the first permanent BBC correspondent in the United States," said Miall, "one of the first chaps I went to seek advice from in what was a new role for me and the BBC, was Ed. In a sense, he was my opposite number."

The essential question he asked Murrow was, simply, how does one act as a radio correspondent in another country? Murrow took Miall to lunch at the Savile Club and there proceeded to offer him a great deal of advice. Murrow first stressed the fundamental tenet that it was necessary to be very careful, extremely careful, to distinguish between reporting the facts and analysis of them. Murrow emphasized that it was the job of the foreign correspondent to provide such analysis and interpretation of the facts of another country, but

> not to breathe in personal comment on them, not to simply give his views on whether it's a good or bad thing, but to explain the significance of this, the translation of it into terms that are readily understandable in one's home country, which hasn't necessarily got the background or the knowledge of the country that you happen to be working in. . . . but to draw a distinction between that and your own personal views, and equally between that and your straight announcement of what has happened.

On a brief return visit to England in 1947, Murrow broadcast on the BBC Home Service a program entitled, "Europe---America's Dilemma." He opened the broadcast with an explanation, almost an apology, for making the talk:

> It has always seemed to me that people who speak on the radio, or the wireless, should present their credentials . . . one whose record and prejudices . . . are to some degree known to the listener.
>
> I am a reporter---like so many Americans, a mixture of English, Scots-Irish and German---a reporter who had the privilege of working here in your island for nine years between 1937 and 1946 . . . not a very long time, not even long enough to write a good book about you . . . . . but long enough to appreciate Emerson's remark, that . . . . the Englishman is "him of all men who stands firmest in his shoes."
>
> This is merely the analysis of one reporter---who has not always been right, but who has not been briefed for this task by officials, either here or in Washington.

The same method that Murrow had so vividly used in England during the war years, in relating events there to his countrymen at home, he later used to help the British understand America. He spoke from experience:

> A few weeks ago I was out in our Middle West---a small town, Peoria in Illinois. This town of fifty thousand is surrounded by flat, black land that produces great corn and wheat crops. The town itself produces a lot of good bourbon whiskey and Caterpillar tractors.
> This town is fifteen hundred miles from salt water, in the heart of what used to be called the isolationist area---but the people there really want to talk about Europe, about your socialist government, about conditions in Italy and France.
> This is a change in attitude, and interest, that was, to this reporter, very remarkable indeed.

The new "internationalism" of the United States had arrived, and Murrow was conveying it to the British in terms of the citizens of Peoria, and Denver, how they were thinking and what they were talking about. He first abstracted down to people, and then would back up to what the big picture really meant. For Murrow, it would probably mean a new national attitude for Americans that would last until the wedge of another war, in far-off Vietnam, twenty years later, would reverse the then-traditional "internationalist" view. But in 1947, as Murrow put it, "On trains, in buses, in wayside inns, the Americans, well fed, wasteful and wondering, are talking about Europe. This is new and different."

In an effort to establish common bonds and relatedness, Murrow went on to explain how the Americans and the British were similar. He had been impressed with the many similarities between the two peoples as a result of his travels between the two countries. He began by pointing out that, "in a curious fashion, we share your dislike of foreigners . . . we share your fondness for pageantry and romance and we share your insistence that the individual shall have the right to be wrong."

And, according to Murrow, Americans were unpredictable. But whose fault was that? "Largely your fault," answered Murrow, "because so many of us stem from so many of you. We, like you, are testy and headstrong, with a certain range and variety of character, wishing neither to command or obey, but to be kings in our own houses." Earlier, back in the States, he broadcast from America to England on the BBC, reversing his wartime role. It was in the heat of that 1947 summer, and he early mentioned to his British audience that, in the dog days of August, it was a "time when we Americans think even less than usual about our own national affairs and the state of the world in which we live."

Comparing President Truman to a Yorkshireman, Murrow was able to make clear to his audience just what kind of leader was in the White House: "Mr. Truman comes from the State of Missouri. The people out there are a little like those in Yorkshire. It isn't enough to 'tell' them; they want to be shown. . . . He, like [Prime Minister Clement] Attlee, would not stand out in a crowd, and no Savile Row tailor would approve the President's suits; they're too tight."

But Murrow recognized openly, on this broadcast, that communication was a difficult job, one that required much experience and thought, however others tried to shorten the process:

> This business of understanding what goes on in the other person's country is not very easy. For example, a certain section of the Press and radio over here has been telling us that a government crisis in Britain is possible, probable, or imminent.
> So far as one can judge at this distance, those reports are the result of a single editorial in a single London newspaper. It's all rather confusing.

And in a satiric mode, he added:

> Last night I was talking with a friend of mine just over from London, who told me that in three days he had found three people over here who had diagnosed all Britain's troubles and recommended a cure. But he hadn't been able to find anybody here who could give him any definitive information how near we were to a depression, whereas in London, he knew several people who could tell him exactly the state of our economy, and when and in what circumstances, the crash would come.

Perhaps we should have more of this long-range diagnosis. It would appear that the further one gets away from problems or crises, the easier it is to identify and diagnose them, or so, at least, many people believe. Finally, in concluding the broadcast, Murrow took cognizance of what his English friends would be doing:

> It just occurred to me that probably not many people are listening to this broadcast. Most of you are probably getting ready to leave for August bank holiday.
> I hope the trains are on time---the pubs don't run dry---and the skies are kind.

Another broadcast to the British from the States can provide additional insights into Murrow's general communication technique. In this broadcast in 1949, he opened with the statement that his commentary would be "lazy" and "unorthodox." Lazy because he had cabled friends in Britain asking what would be of interest to them, so all he had to do was answer their questions; unorthodox "because I am acutely conscious that I am talking from a land that is fat, to a land that is lean, and because I propose to make this a rather personal report to friends with whom I spent the grim and glorious years between 1937 and 1946."

These scripts seem almost an effort to "break away" from his "home" environment to which he had triumphantly returned after nine years in Europe. They appear to be an attempt at working-out, or thinking-out, his "cultural shock."

In another broadcast, he discussed the Marshall Plan and the newly-enacted Taft-Hartley Act. Giving a clue as to his ideological wellsprings, he interpreted the latter as follows: "In the last couple of weeks, labor has lost many of the gains it made during the last couple of decades." Going on, Murrow looked at differences that divided the two countries: "Your economic future baffles our economists; your military security concerns our militarists; your financial situation puzzles our financiers. The political philosophy of your government frightens some of our conservatives." Interestingly, these comments are probably still appropriate in the latter part of the 1970s decade.

Then, Murrow talked of our national holiday, the Fourth of July. He said that there would be a lot of oratory and there would be picnics, and people eating sand in sandwiches, and many well-fed people eating more than was good for them. And he felt that it would be very difficult for many Americans to understand what was happening in Europe. Expressing his belief in the learning that experience only can provide, he exclaimed, "It is difficult to explain the meaning of cold to people who are warm, the meaning of privation to people who have wanted only for luxuries. . . . It is almost impossible to substitute intelligence for experience." These perspicacious and prophetic words describe with great accuracy the growing tendency today to withdraw from the problems of the world as a rich and overfed America grows increasingly indifferent to poverty and hunger in the Third World.

In the eloquent ending of this broadcast, Murrow told the British that, of all American holidays, the Fourth of July was theirs as well:

> This holiday of ours tomorrow is part of your tradition, your folklore, just as it is part of the mythology by which we live.
>
> For you have exported over much of the world people who demanded independence, tolerance and the right to be wrong.
>
> For the last few days I've been looking around for something we both share, something which is not new, neither a plan nor a doctrine, but rather something that says in common language a common conviction.
>
> The search for such a combination of words has taken me back to the Fourth of July, 1940, when my New York office instructed me to proceed to Dover and prepare broadcasts for the Fourth of July. You will remember the circumstances. It was a time when most men save British despaired of Britain's life. I felt that no words of mine would have real meaning to people at home. After all, it was the Fourth of July . . . .

I came back to words that were uttered in the House of Commons in 1775. . . . 'Slavery they can have anywhere; it is a weed that grows in every soil. They may have it from Spain; they may have it from Prussia. But until you become lost to all feeling of your true interest and your national dignity, freedom they can have from none but you. This is the commodity of price of which you have the monopoly.'

Those words were uttered by Edmund Burke.

Yes, Murrow needed time on the air to roam around, to dig into and work out his subject. Radio was his medium for analysis and thought in specifics about people and the cultures they fostered. His forte was not moralizing nor inner soul-baring nor existential mysticism, but an attempt to explain to others, clearly and concisely, what he himself understood. This simple description provides a key to understanding the philosophy of communication and the art of broadcast journalism as developed by Edward R. Murrow. Its success, as we shall see, lay not only in his receiving the plaudits of the famous and the acclaim of the masses, but in the success of the approach as an educational tool to awaken, enlighten, and transform the public into aware, participating members of a democratic society. Not perfectly, of course, but in a different and more effective way than was true in the past.

CHAPTER VIII

ARTIST AT THE MICROPHONE

If the fairly abstract "radio" was the medium of Murrow's message, then the microphone was certainly its concrete instrument and weapon. That small piece of metal meant a great deal to Ed Murrow, and he was awed by its power. True to what we have learned about his technological ignorance, Murrow once said: "To this reporter all microphones look alike." Even so, he regarded the microphone as "the most revealing instrument devised by the hand of man---an accurate mirror of prejudice and bigotry, as well as honesty." And what was important was the other end of this communication chain. He never lost sight of the *purpose* of speaking into the microphone: "You must remember that the only thing that's important in broadcasting is what comes out of the loudspeaker, and not the plans and schemes that are concocted in comfortable offices."

As members of the radio audience, we all heard the results of Murrow's work. And one reason why he was effective was the "conscious act" by which he approached that microphone. Frank Gillard, former BBC Correspondent and Director of Sound Broadcasting, has noted that Murrow told him once that "The good broadcaster never for a moment takes his mind off his words, even if the words are there before him on a sheet of paper. He thinks his way through his script, even if he knows it by heart."[1]

Michael Standing, also a wartime BBC correspondent and colleague of Murrow's, was most impressed with the CBS Director's ability to ad-lib in a highly descriptive way. Standing said that the BBC had long considered the problem of summoning up for people the imaginative processes which allow them to see an event as they hear it, even though the difficulty was a relatively new one. The on-the-spot report that gave the radio reporter a golden opportunity to "paint pictures" in peoples' minds came into its own only during the war.

The initial task, thought Standing, was to bring the audience immediately up to date about an event that was taking place before the eyes of the commentator. For Standing, this meant that "This had to be done quickly, it had to be done in short, telling phrases, and it had to bring them to the point that the commentator could then develop from, as the event unfolded before him."

The problem, however, was that most broadcasters just took too long a time in recapping what had happened, not staying with the story. "Ed seemed to have a mastery of this," Standing remarked. "I think he was an instinctive commentator in that way, relying on his descriptive capacity, on a good vocabulary, on a clear choice of words, but above all, a capacity to cope with the event as it

---

[1]Frank Gillard's comments about Edward R. Murrow are based on a letter from him to the author, dated July 21, 1970.

developed, rather than a capacity to rehearse what had happened in the sense of a reporter telling the story." And, if there were difficulties in keeping up with the developing event, Murrow "would simply not cover up when his own knowledge of an event was insufficient to allow himself to describe it accurately." He would say so, which was also an engaging characteristic, Standing felt, especially since he would admit it "not in the kind of cliche-ridden way that some of us did when we rather made fools of ourselves, but in a way that was so transparently honest and direct that it engaged sympathy and goodwill rather than irritation and general annoyance."

Godfrey Talbot, also a BBC war correspondent, spoke of Murrow's delivery as something of a treat, as a delight to the ear:

> Perhaps he was ordinary in the States. To us, he was fascinating in his own talk because of the slickness of his talk, the polish of his talk, the iconoclasm of his talk; he would knock things down, bore through things with his talk.

But, Talbot emphasized, in spite of an ability to tell a story smoothly and slickly, Murrow was a "very sensitive man; very much a human being able to be touched by other people's experiences." These qualities were not contradictory, according to Talbot: "One of the great qualities of Ed Murrow was, he was able---almost with a professional naivete---to absorb scenes, sounds, experiences of himself and others, and present them in all their reality and stark simplicity." Without the use of any pictures, Murrow's forte was what he could do with the spoken word. Talbot elaborated:

> He was able through the spoken word . . . to give you a picture of what it felt like, what it smelt like, what it burned like and what it was like, at the time, on the spot. So you the listener were standing with him, you were beside him at the microphone, in the streets of London. You were with him in the studio.

And he did it succinctly. "The economy of adjective, of word" was the way he was able to make things real, according to Talbot, to present pictures through the ear, "as real as anything that television nowadays gives."

Talbot added that Murrow had the true skill of the narrator in that he didn't have to embellish, but rather to simplify: "His ability to simplify and throw away the frills and the journalistic flim-flam was one of his great merits."

Talbot didn't choose to say whether Murrow was more talented at ad-lib commentary or in the studio with a scripted news broadcast. He was simply good at both, Talbot reminisced:

> He would of course go out with the microphone; his voice would come through the noise of the bombs, and wail of the fire engines, ringing of the bells and so on. He did both, you see; he never pretended, in the studio, that he was somewhere else.

It was scripted, and well scripted. When he was doing an outside broadcast, ad-libbing a spontaneous commentary, then it was clearly that. He was good at both.

To us also, it was something of the voice of doom. I don't mean the voice of doom in that he was giving evil tidings to us; this was the voice that was unsparing of our emotions, the voice that told dire tidings because Ed believed to tell the direst of tidings and the worst that was happening was to get to the truth.

This was the voice of a man who didn't spare himself or us anything, and of course the timbre of the voice was deep and penetrating; it was abrasive, if you like. There was no honey and wine and cigars about Ed's voice.

It punched through; it was the voice of doom, not the end, but the voice of dire tidings.

It was one of these good, virile North American voices which wake you out of any sleep you might have listening to the wireless.

At times Murrow's was a voice of doom that brought bad tidings because, according to Talbot, it was a way to get at the truth. Or, couched in the modern terms that have been debated by media, audience, and government of late, "Bad news is news in a basically good society." Or, as Eric Sevareid once said, "You can always find good news in Spain or Russia." Perhaps the "direst of tidings" was easier to accept in a simpler world of the "Allies" united against the "Axis." The cry of today's world is: "Kill the messenger bringing bad omens," as a vast variety of changing and complex issues divide peoples into bitter camps.

Talbot summarized with simplicity: "What, essentially, that man was doing was being Mr. Ordinary; he wasn't being Mr. Anybody Special. That was his great gift. It was the great gift of any good spoken-word reporter."

Writer D. G. Bridson remembers watching Murrow work before the microphone. There was always "sort of an ironic smile on his face." Murrow, to Bridson, was sort of "rangy, gaunt, a humorous character." And on the air:

He used his hands to emphasize what he was talking about. Particularly, of course, it was his voice. I don't know how to describe his voice. The nearest thing I think I can get to it, is a really incisive version of Jimmy Stewart, the film actor.

The last person you'd associate with Ed in any other way. But simply the timbre of the voice. If it had had more edge on it and not been so . . . so . . . quite so thick . . . had it been sharper, brisker, edgier, it would not have been unlike Ed's.

It should be pointed out here that the use Murrow made of his voice was not totally intuitive and automatic. This was not an area of his work at which he arrived totally untrained. He had had formal speech training at Washington State College and

Ida Lou Anderson, his speech teacher there, remained a constant critic and listener throughout the war years. All the evidence tends to indicate that Murrow prized her comments; he was devoted to his former instructor.

Eric Sevareid remembered that his former boss was not always understanding toward his staff in matters of actual broadcasting: "He'd get upset about certain things I'd do or say, or maybe a certain broadcast." And, Sevareid added with a pained expression of confession, "I was a terrible broadcaster in the early radio days. I never had a speech lesson in my life, but Ed was very accomplished at that."

A qualification should be mentioned. Ed Murrow did not always sound smooth, authoritative, and flawless on the air, speech training or no. Listening to recorded segments of broadcasts from very early in the war at the BBC Sound Archives, one realizes that Murrow took time to mature in his delivery. In a broadcast as late as March of 1942, Murrow narrated a program called "Three Years of War." His voice was rather tense and high-pitched by comparison with later broadcasts. Strangely, his delivery was also singsong, in a regular rising/falling pattern not necessarily connected to the meaning. It seems likely that he did not write this particular narration.

In other broadcasts, one can occasionally hear what bothers most of us in speaking: "uhs" and "aas" between phrases. In one broadcast, his voice sounded distant---foggy and painfully fatigued. The broadcast was obviously made while he was ill. In his broadcast delivery, Ed Murrow was very human, and perhaps not as consistently effective in his earliest years as he became later on.

Murrow was very human, indeed, in suffering the agony of "mike fright," a phenomenon as old as radio, and one that all public performers, it seems, must suffer in order to be effective. How many actors have testified to their unease after many hundreds of performances? (The late Basil Rathbone once said that it had to be, for "without stage fright, a performance is nothing.") The tension, the adrenalin: these are what added electricity to Murrow's microphone technique.

Two close colleagues and witnesses, Charles Collingwood and Eric Sevareid, bear this out. Both men testified to the fact that heavy perspiration was characteristic of Murrow when he was broadcasting. Collingwood said:

> Ed was the only man I ever knew who sweated more than I do. And in an English studio, even a chilly one---and English studios during the war were not overheated---the intensity with which he broadcast, although it never sounded that way, caused rivulets of sweat.

This, it seemed, was a permanent condition:

> This persisted all his life, and in television studios, in between takes, during the commercial, the make-up girl would come racing in and dab him down with a

cloth or kleenex or whatever. They'd have to do that to
me. I'm the same way. But Ed, always, in a broadcast,
would perspire heavily.

Was the perspiration an indication of tension and mike fright? Collingwood was confident that it was:

It certainly was tension, and besides that, the tension would be revealed the way his knee would jiggle; his knee and foot would jiggle up and down while he was broadcasting. And perhaps this accounts for the feeling of urgency.

Collingwood added that the power of the broadcasts came from a totality of energy that Murrow put into them. It wasn't a question of diction or vocal technique, although these were handled with artistry. It was, rather, "because of the manner of his delivery which had a kind of concentration of all his energies in it. It had nothing to do with being hysterical or raising your voice or anything else. It has just to do with the input of energy."

Eric Sevareid has said that Murrow never betrayed nervousness in his broadcasts, although he did suffer mike fright, as nearly everyone does. Sevareid felt that he himself suffered the worst of all: "My symptom of 'mike fright' was the worst one, which was shortness of breath. I couldn't breathe properly. I remember my father was the same way. Ed's symptom was heavy sweating." And the knee action as well:

He'd have one knee over the other, and his feet would be going like this---up and down---as be broadcast. Other people would get butterflies in the belly or weak at the knees or something. I never had those symptoms. I just couldn't speak properly because my breath would grow short, and that's the worst possible symptom.
   He never had that. He had this complete control of his breathing and his voice. But he'd sweat like a pig. It would just pour off him, roll down his cheek.
   These live radio broadcasts, we'd all have to relax. It was an effort. He'd gear himself up to it. Don't think he ever did a broadcast easily and in a relaxed way.

Two broadcasts which Murrow did are now so well known that they are classic examples of what can be called "radio literature." They are included in any anthology or selected excerpts of Murrow scripts. They were printed, at the time, in London papers. One was the "Berlin is an orchestrated hell" broadcast, describing just what it was like to take part in a raid over a beseiged city of an enemy. The other was his report on Buchenwald in 1945, which he visited the day of President Roosevelt's death.

It would be redundant to reprint here those scripts (available in Edward Bliss's collection, *In Search of Light*,[2] and elsewhere). Reading them would shed little light on how Murrow broadcast them, how he felt, his temperament at the time. Fortunately, there were witnesses, in the studio at the time they were delivered, who can recall those broadcasts. They can add at least some enlightenment on how Murrow reacted under the stress and tension of broadcasting two of the most powerful reports ever transmitted by radio.

Eric Sevareid remembers how Murrow always preferred to be in the air rather than on the ground:

> He loved airplanes and loved speed. He loved the danger and thrill of that. He was not happy on the ground, with infantry. . . . I'd rather be with a rifle company as a journalist than on airplanes. I couldn't stand them.

(To understand why, one has only to read Sevareid's account in *Not So Wild a Dream* of what it was like to bail out of a doomed aircraft over unknown territory.)

Sevareid was in London when Murrow went on the big bombing raid over Berlin, in which Bob Post of the *New York Times* was lost. A massive raid, a night raid. After the raid and Murrow's return, Sevareid listened to the broadcast in the studio. He described what happened:

> When Ed came back he hadn't slept for a couple of days and nights. He came into the studio, and he had a big drink of whiskey.
> An utterly exhausted man, and yet, they were live broadcasts; you didn't tape things.
> The light came up, he went through this broadcast, his voice as strong as ever, and he did an eloquent, brilliant piece about this raid.
> And then he just simply collapsed. An empty shell.

Perhaps a brief reminder about the Buchenwald broadcast is in order. He began by telling how he was traveling through a confused Germany. He noted that the Germans seemed to be in good condition, but warned his audience that "this is no time to talk about the surface of Germany." If they were listening and it was lunchtime, this would not be pleasant. The body of the broadcast was largely interviews he had had in the death camp with survivors and doctors, along with his own observations. From what he saw, he concluded:

> There was a German trailer which must have contained another fifty [bodies], but it wasn't possible to count them. The clothing was piled in a heap against the wall.

---

[2]Edward Bliss, Jr., ed., *In Search of Light---The Broadcasts of Edward R. Murrow 1938-1961* (New York: Alfred A. Knopf, 1967).

It appeared that most of the men and boys had died of starvation; they had not been executed.
But the manner of death seemed unimportant. Murder had been done at Buchenwald.

Toward the end of that broadcast, one hears his voice crack slightly. Clearly he was near weeping as he referred to the death of Roosevelt and what FDR's life meant to the inmates of the camp. Murrow concluded:

> At Buchenwald, they spoke of him [Roosevelt] just before he died. If there be a better epitaph, history does not record it.
> For years, FDR . . . meant the full measure of their hope. Chuchill said to me in 1941, with tears in his eyes, 'One day, the world and history will recognize and acknowledge what it owes to your President.'
> I saw and heard the first installment of that at Buchenwald on Thursday.

This is only the second recording in which the author heard Murrow's voice break. The other was his closed-circuit farewell to CBS affiliates when he left the network to head the United States Information Agency in 1961. Again, someone was there in the studio to hear Murrow give that broadcast. D. G. Bridson has recalled: "I think that when he came back from Buchenwald, he had been terribly shaken by what he saw in that concentration camp. I never saw him so cut up by anything; he was really sort of trembling. Yes literally."

Bridson said that Murrow had been back only two or three hours, that he had flown back to prepare and deliver his broadcast:

> He just went into the studio and told what he had seen. You might say that what he said was objective, but my God, his reaction to what he had seen was as subjective as all hell.
> He was shaking with rage by the time he finished it. There was no question of "let's not be beastly to the Germans." What he had seen, he wanted the world to know.
> Something which he would get across to the starry-eyed listener who thought, "Oh, well, that's a long way away, doesn't really have anything to do with us."
> Well, Ed was just in a mood to kick them right in the teeth. That was one of the most notable newscasts of his that I ever heard.

Most of the time, with forceful calm, Murrow approached the microphone with respect, thinking and working his way through his script with great intensity. Sweat falling, knee bobbing, hand moving---his entire being was concentrated in that small interval of time as he summoned all energies to communicate with his audience. Only rarely---as in the Buchenwald broadcast---did his inner turmoil break through the surface.

CHAPTER IX

ARTIST OF ORAL LANGUAGE

Sitting with headphones on, listening to those crackling, static-filled records and tapes at Broadcast House, one sensed almost immediately a characteristic of Murrow's broadcasts that had never before been appreciated. He possessed the qualities of a storyteller, and when the event was a scene, a place to visit, an on-the-spot occurrence, he was a master of descriptive commentary. Metaphor, personification, crisp short phrases dominated these scenes. And, in a sense, "You Were There."

Certainly Murrow's language always tended toward clarity and detail. When it came to a choice between analysis of a crisis in the British economy or a description of a raid on Berlin, the raid on Berlin had to be the winner.

In considering a man who felt strongly about radio and related to it more than he did to any other medium, it is not inconsistent to suggest he was a storyteller. For what else is radio if not a medium for the imagination? That radio is so seldom used in this manner in the United States today does not detract from its ability to be used in this way.

Ed Murrow, taking off in a plane at sunset, did not say, "The sun is setting." Rather, he described a scene of "rivers and lakes of fire atop the clouds." Bombs fell, if they were small ones, "like a fistful of white rice thrown on a piece of black velvet." Bigger bombs went off "like great sunflowers gone mad." And looking down on a burned Berlin, he saw fires that merged and spread "just like butter on a hot plate."

And what was the meaning of bombs and war? In language eloquent in its simplicity, when he returned from the gigantic Berlin raid, he reported:

> My mind went back to the time I had crossed that coast in 1938, in a plane that had taken off from Prague. Just ahead of me sat two refugees from Vienna---an old man and his wife. The co-pilot came back and told them that we were outside German territory. The old man reached out and grasped his wife's hand.
> The work that was done last night was a massive blow of retribution for all those who have fled from the sound of shots and blows on the stricken continent.

Some of his phrases merely presented small detail that he caught out of the corner of his eye. As he once approached a plane at a landing field, for example, he noted that "a lone hawk hovered over the aircraft." And, occasionally, a particular phrase could be repeated. Speaking to the British in 1946, he said to them: "You came into your full inheritance in 1939," and it was a testing time when the "English dug deep into their history." Just eight years later, in denouncing Senator Joseph McCarthy as a demagogue, he would say, "We will not walk in fear, one of another. We will not be driven by fear into an age of unreason if we dig deep in our history and our doctrine." And, on the same fateful broadcast, "As a nation we have come into our full inheritance at a tender age."

Moreover, Ed Murrow never forgot his audience. In describing an American election to the British, he spoke "British." A lapel button was about the size of "half a crown;" the activity at a meeting was similar to the "pub;" and Times Square, he informed his audience, was the "Piccadilly Circus of New York." In describing a British event to an American audience, he reversed his similes.

Murrow's scripts are available, and they may be read, at least many of them, as a kind of literature. They stand above many of those of his peers as highly esteemed works of art in the records of the mass media. We cannot here make a thorough analysis of all the literary qualities and examples from his many scripts. Perhaps it would be a worthy undertaking, but one that would be done only in the realization that nothing less than tomes would result--- that is, if the job were done competently.

Those observers who worked with and near him could add their personal reflections on his language style, and, taken together, could give better insights into his use of words.

His pungency of phrases and forcefulness particularly fitted a time of war, thought Sir Lindsay Wellington, because brutal things were happening, "or things which were shrouded in mists, that were veiled." Sir Lindsay was close at hand while Murrow broadcast from London, and also later when he himself was in New York, hearing the broadcasts as Americans did.

"Ed was a great master of the short sentence and the brilliant but not flashy use of words," commented Sir Lindsay. He felt that Murrow never would have "looked as well on paper as he sounded on the air." That was because he thought in terms of short sentences, concrete images, colorful words, all of which Sir Lindsay felt were the ingredients for bringing radio broadcasts to life: "If you're not going to use those sorts of approaches, if you're going in for purple passages, for romantic rhetoric, for moving people by those means, well . . . you'd better be Churchill." For Churchill broke every rule that any producer had ever conceived, but obviously got away with it. Sir Lindsay has reminded the world that it was Murrow himself who said of Churchill, "He mobilized the English language and made it fight."

Sir Lindsay was not at all quizzical about Murrow's desire for a longer newscast than, say, Elmer Davis had. He felt that Davis polished his craft to fit the particular challenge, namely, to try to convey what he could in five minutes. But Murrow needed more room to roam around:

The Bible or the secret of Beethoven can't be told in two minutes. And if Ed was---and I think he was---often talking of those subjects, he did need more time, more space to move in, to develop and reveal thinking.

Not literally on those subjects, of course, but involved and complex analyses of the success or failure of a German blockade, or a campaign in which subtle judgments had to be made after sifting and winnowing through a mountain of facts. Almost as an aside, Sir Lindsay once remarked that Ed Murrow, *by necessity*, was able to handle the short, crisp broadcast.

To Thomas Barman, Murrow was "an uninhibited chap talking." He broadcast in the present tense very early in the war, while the BBC broadcasts, long before American broadcasts, were often recorded. Immediacy is the prime asset for bringing the news home; there is a certain staleness in the after-the-fact broadcast. Certainly, too, a "chap talking" is in the greatest tradition of the spoken word of radio.

The "essence" of the story was still the important thing, according to Michael Standing. Regardless of color or imagery or conversational style, Standing noted that the "essential factors were broadcast in the opening paragraph" and that after the first fifteen or twenty lines came the argument, the detail, and the comment. In some instances, Murrow did seem to follow this longstanding pattern of journalistic reporting. On other occasions, however, he worked into the report in an almost leisurely way, introducing the subject or setting the scene.

Leonard Miall summed up Murrow's literary talent: Stylistically, he wrote well. In simple, clear sentences in the active, not passive sense." But he didn't simply read his copy, he "really rethought what he had written in front of the microphone. That was one of his skills. He also had a lovely voice."

A sparing use of adjectives gave the few that he used real impact, thought Godfrey Talbot: "Ed was the master of the flat, apparently flat but carefully worded statement, unadorned with frills." Whenever he would use an adjective, it came with all the punch in the world because it was a rare one. Said Talbot: "He was lean of figure and his prose was lean."

Talbot thought that Murrow's style truly represented his purposes. He wanted to tell people what war was *really* like, not "at the pithead but at the cold face, not at headquarters but at the front line." He was never doing a broadcast "performance" or trying to be a clever personality. He was, rather, trying to tell somebody in the simplest possible terms, in the most truthful and succinct terms, what had happened in a given situation. Said Talbot: "His broadcasts had all the exaggeration of underemphasis." This description probably sums up Murrow's style more aptly than any other ever made about it. Power through the sparing use of words and underplay was *the* stylistic approach that characterized most of Murrow's broadcasts.

"He had a clear idea of what he wanted to say, and a very clear idea of the best way of saying it." That's how writer D. G. Bridson looks at Murrow's style. It was in a word, "incisive."

And through his words, carefully chosen, he could make his listeners not only understand what he was talking about, but make them feel a part of it as well.

While Murrow disliked sentiment and a "cornball" approach to events repelled him, there were times when Murrow could lapse into sentimentality. "There were broadcasts of his that were pretty corny, now that you look back at them, though in a wartime atmosphere you don't feel that as much." That was how colleague Eric Sevareid put it. Reiterating what others in the trade have said, Sevareid indicated that there was nothing academic about Murrow or his writing. He made everything "concrete." Sevareid noted, "You read those scripts of that time, and everything's specific. He knew that trick of writing instinctively. He got down to the bare bones of things."

Murrow got down to the concrete, bare details, to capture the "feel" not only of an event, but of a people as well. Former BBC War Correspondent Robert Reid, when queried about Murrow's broadcast "style," chuckled as he told one story that Ed Murrow had reported from the field in North Africa that Reid thought was so representative of British manners and style. And Murrow brought it home just that way.

A small town had been liberated as a result of that seemingly endless desert campaign, and Murrow was there with a British public relations officer to report the event. The officer was a personal friend of Reid's, a tall cavalry officer, a baronet---the fifteenth baronet in his line. Murrow reported the scene. The tall officer leaned down from his great height, resting on his walking stick, calmly listening to a local North African chief delivering an impassioned address to him. When the chief finished, there was silence for a moment, and then the cavalry officer said, simply, "Too true, Chum, too true." "The way Ed put it over, all his friends recognized the officer," said Reid. "This was perfect, you see."

It was that kind of true to life reporting that led many of his colleagues to refer to Ed Murrow, with great respect, as an "artist of oral language." Ed, however, never thought of himself in this way, preferring to believe that his approach was simply one of letting people and events speak for themselves. From his own perspective, this was the best way to sum up his "broadcast style."

CHAPTER X

ARTIST WITHOUT PEER

Why, one might ask, is Edward R. Murrow associated in the public mind, and with his colleagues in the broadcast profession as well, so emphatically with the dramatic and effective reporting of the war from his English base. After all, there were others who broadcast, who had talent, who lost sleep, who were daring. Murrow's own staff was made up of dedicated and skilled reporters, and there were other networks with efficient staffs and reporters as well. Despite the fact that there were, indeed, many other Americans around Broadcast House during that time of the blitz and war, history tends to single out Edward R. Murrow as the master reporter or recorder of events. Why? Was it simply superior talent? Was it timing? Was it a kind of personal magnetism?

These are questions which led to the interviewing of numerous BBC personnel in an effort to seek answers, for it is evident that, during the war, Murrow reigned supreme in the estimation of British colleagues and listeners over other radio reporters from the United States. Murrow's picture is on the cover of Asa Briggs' history of the BBC during the war years, along with a very small number of important British broadcasting figures. Murrow moreso than any other American reporter is referred to with great frequency in that book. In Briggs' view, Murrow seems to have been an integral part of the BBC wartime story.

Murrow's status, however, was in another sense not so special, according to retired diplomatic correspondent Thomas Barman. Barman, who served in the British Government's propaganda department for the first three years of the war, reported that all British authorities, but especially Winston Churchill and Brendan Bracken, wartime Minister of Information, made a great fuss over all American correspondents: "They were treated as tin gods, all of them, because they were so useful."

Barman saw the situation as one in which the Prime Minister and Minister of Information, in the interest of strengthening the war effort against Hitler, had to make themselves available to all correspondents whenever feasible. BBC records, however, reveal some instances when Murrow had comparatively little difficulty getting permission to go on air raids or similar assignments, as compared with other reporters. In some cases, it may have been a matter of others having less experience on the job. "Certainly," felt Barman, "the British government did something to build up the personalities of these people." He offered Quentin Reynolds as another example of a correspondent to whom much deference was shown. Together, Murrow, Reynolds, and a few others were the "pampered picks" of the top leaders. This evaluation by Barman, it should be noted, must be viewed from the perspective that the British government needed the most capable spokesmen to get its position across to the American public.

In time of war, Barman later philosophized, everyone gets chances he otherwise would not get. One's work becomes more important; people have a cause, a dedication: "The junior clerk in an office suddenly called upon to do some sort of clerical work for some government department is quite a different being than a junior clerk in a mercer's [clothing] office."

The wartime atmosphere obviously explains, at least in part, Murrow's rise to prominence. Barman, however, has noted that he does not think that Murrow stood out above other American correspondents later in the war: "I think he stood out particularly in 1940 and 1941 during the blitz." Murrow was able to bring the full horrors of the war scene home to the American public; Britain was alone, and desperately needed a powerful friend. By comparison, Barman believed, others just didn't do this part of the job as well. In a subtle way, Barman appears to regard Murrow as the most effective propagandist for the British cause with the American public during this early war period.

But what changed after 1940 and 1941? According to Barman: "Well, the blitz was over; it was a steady slogging war after that. Much steadier war, until you got the buzz bombs." Still, when pressed, Barman acknowledged the great contribution that Murrow made to the total war effort throughout the war years, conceding that he was a most persuasive man with a beautiful voice and a certain charisma. In summing up, Barman stated that in the early stages of the war, Murrow contributed immensely to an American awareness of Britain's plight and, perhaps, did indeed do it better than others.

But why? What was it about Murrow that enabled him to stand out amongst a group of radio broadcasters most of whom were already famous or were destined to be acclaimed in the future? Barmon sought to offer an explanation:

[Ed Murrow had] a war personality, a convincing personality, and [was] a man whose heart was in the right place. It all came out of that. Others may have been just as good, but they didn't come over the same way. . . . they lacked something.

When asked if these remarks related to the subject of communication, Barman replied: "Yes, and Ed Murrow had it in the highest degree." But there was a qualifier, and it involved timing. "You've got to be a good communicator," Barman insisted, "but at the right time! . . . I doubt if either Churchill or Murrow could have communicated much in 1935."

Leonard Miall, who has had a long and illustrious career with the BBC, confirmed that Murrow was able to get things which others could not get---at least, no other BBC reporter. In effect, Churchill said that if Murrow wanted to go on a particular assignment, then he was to be sent. It was important to the British that their story be told, and Murrow was superb at telling it in the right way.

"A matter of timing" seemed prominent in D. G. Bridson's evaluation of why Murrow stood above the rest. This wartime writer and producer for the BBC thought it was because Murrow was first, on the scene at the beginning. Murrow was extremely valuable to the British for his reporting of the blitz to America. He was, according to Bridson, very much "persona grata" with the authorities. Had others come along first, perhaps they too would have had the doors opened, and might have made a similar impression. But Murrow was the man in the position, and "luckily he was the right man in the position."

Bridson went on to add that of course Murrow's talents placed him at the top of the list. Bridson noted that European dispatches would come in from about thirty British, twelve American, and two or three Canadian correspondents. In preparing the half-hour program "War Report," the best of the day's reports were selected, and a lot of Murrow's material was used. This was not because it was a question of obliging American correspondents, but "because he was a darn sight better than any of the people we'd got at the time in that particular area."

In seeking other responses as to why Murrow stood above other American reporters, words like "integrity" and "conviction" seemed to come up again and again. To Leonard Miall, Murrow's youthful upbringing had a lot to do with it. The best elaboration of that comment is found in Alexander Kendrick's *Prime Time*, in the story of Murrow's childhood in the Pacific Northwest, wherein Kendrick concludes that "it really was a question of personal integrity."

There were many people who could observe an event and narrate what happened, who could master the facts and figures, and do a good job of handling them. But it was the special ingredient of "conviction" that made the difference, according to Sir Lindsay Wellington: "The taste and savour of Ed's performance was different from theirs [other correspondents and broadcasters] most of the time. How do you define this conviction? I felt it. That's all I can say."

In addition to Murrow's language and vocal talents, according to Michael Standing, "I think he probably was a more dedicated person than most of us, because he had firm and clear and thought-out convictions." Murrow would not interpret events in an easy and unthinking way. There was a special gloss involving explanation and commentary that he would have, one that would commend itself to leaders of the nation and thinking politicians.

The ability to "read" people and relate to them was the main difference, according to Michael Balkwill. That and Murrow's tireless efforts on the job. He felt that Murrow took extra pains in his work, searching out currents of opinion and experiencing events for himself. Support this with a fine mind and prose style and a "first-class broadcasting manner," and you have an exceptional correspondent. "Brilliance is not too great a word to use, I think."

He was simply in a class by himself. Balkwill agreed that there were other competent reporters, or "craftsmen," who were agreeable people to meet and who had knowledge of the job. But Murrow's dealings with people were simply "impressive."

Murrow made you feel that he was vitally interested in you, Balkwill has commented, and he had a unique talent for conversation with others; yet, at the same time, he got the facts that he wanted. He never interviewed; he conversed. And since he was able to talk to so many different kinds of people so well, he gained a fund of reaction from them, and he had readily available a large reservoir of opinion and attitudes.

In his autobiography, Eric Sevareid was eloquent in speaking of Murrow's special talents:

> Of the American journalists who did more than their technical duty, none reached the stature of Murrow, whose physical, intellectual, and moral performance in those deadly weeks is not likely to be equaled by any reportorial voice or pen in this generation.

Sevareid said that Murrow had a hard core of "integrity" which no man, no matter how powerful or persuasive, could chip. In a personal insight vivid in its description of the man and what he could bring to his work, Sevareid summed up:

> He was a complex of strong, simple faiths and refined, sophisticated intellectual processes---poet and preacher, sensitive artist and hard-bitten, poker-playing diplomat, an engaging boy one moment and an unknowable recluse the next, a man who liked people in general and loved a few whom he held off at arm's length.

Part of Murrow's strength lay in the performance of little thoughtful acts that others neglected. As already noted, Cecilia Reeves remembered Murrow as the only correspondent who bothered to call Jan Masaryk at the time of Munich and the carving-up of Czechoslovakia.

Robin Duff was quite blunt about it. In comparing Murrow with his colleague from NBC, Duff said, without malice or criticism, "Oh, you never thought about Fred [Bate] and Ed at the same time in the same way. He [Fred] was an office manager, administrator, not really a broadcaster."

One person was even more blunt, and that was Godfrey Talbot, former BBC War Correspondent. When it was suggested to Talbot that he had perhaps regarded Murrow in a separate class from other American reporters, his face hardened. Slowly, with firm emphasis on each word, Talbot churned out the words: "Other American correspondents were little men!"

Talbot explained that he meant this only in a relative sense. There were all degrees of talent, character, and stature. And he said that there were other American reporters doing a good job. But Ed stood alone. Why? Talbot explained: "I think he was outstanding because of the fire that burned inside of him." A burning drive to get and tell the story, and, like a laser beam, his energy focused on this goal until, in the end, he burned himself out. With those words, Godfrey Talbot probably best explained why Edward R. Murrow has been, and still can be described as "artist without peer" and dean of the Allied war correspondents.

CHAPTER XI

THE DOUGHTY ANGLOPHILE

It is worthwhile to come to grips with Edward R. Murrow's attitudes toward the British, what he achieved or hoped to achieve in his work with them, and what the British---both governmental officials and general public---felt he contributed. During the nine-year span he was in Great Britain, Murrow got to know the British well, and he came to understand their character and their problems.

The English tend to react mildly or even with tentative agreement to a rude or critical comment. You don't argue or even disagree with someone until you know him fairly well. This, anyway, is how one Englishman, Sir Lindsay Wellington, has described one common trait of his countrymen. It was a trait that bothered Ed Murrow mightily in the early prewar days when he first arrived in England. According to Sir Lindsay, "I tried to give him a certain amount of argument just to please him." He would get rather angry with the English because they wouldn't stand up and argue. In turn, Murrow "liked to come out with fairly firm, very crisp, very clear, rather surprising judgments. He got a great deal of fun out of that." The process of argument was a good way to get new ideas and to test one's own. And that, implied Sir Lindsay, was at least part of Murrow's motivation to argue, along with his appreciation for the sheer fun of the mental exercise. Putting it another way, Sir Lindsay said,

> He disliked, in the early days, what he would call the sort of plummy facade of the educated British who, as he thought, would shy away from a good he-man argument, those whose public manners were different from the ones he wanted them to have, in other words.

Later, Sir Lindsay noted, Murrow would have chuckled at his early attitude, after he had spent many long hours in verbal battles with Britons whom he found "not as mealy-mouthed as he had first thought." It was refreshing to hear that there was anything at all that Murrow disliked about the British, for he was truly an Anglophile. He loved the people, the country, and its traditions. Most particularly, he loved the strength of its people in time of adversity. Charles Collingwood once said that Murrow greatly admired the staunchness of their character and their ability to withstand many unpleasant things and still maintain their sense of humor. This character trait was by no means reserved for the leaders of the country, but Murrow related it to the little fellow as well, who could crawl out of the ruins of his bombed house and make a joke of it.

He also, according to Collingwood, admired the good manners of the British, and their articulateness, including that of the Irish: "I remember once he and I were in Dublin together. He loved the marvelous way the Irish could talk of an evening, especially over a glass of whiskey, to which he was by no means averse." Although Murrow thought that the British---even moreso than the Irish---were the best conversationalists in the world, Collingwood wasn't so certain that this was true. He also thought that Murrow was overly impressed with the absolute refusal of the British people to admit the possibility of defeat in the war, even though that possibility was a strong one, especially in 1940 and 1941. Except for a few sophisticates, it is not in the British character to admit that things are hopeless. Whether this was a weakness or a delusion, Murrow thought the British ability to "muddle through," as the phrase went in those days, was indeed a considerable virtue.

Collingwood stressed that until the end of his days Murrow had an enormous fondness for the British, and he came back to visit the country whenever he could. The British reciprocated his affection. Collingwood has recalled participating in the special broadcasts on BBC radio and television and on independent television at the time of Murrow's death. He recalled especially a poignant story that portrays the respect with which the British regarded Murrow, even twenty years after the war. Collingwood was going into the House of Commons, and the police officer at the gate recognized him. The officer commented with obvious respect: "I know you. You were Ed Murrow's mate." Collingwood said the man was a very young person and couldn't possibly have known much about World War II: "But 'Murrow,' Ed Murrow's name and personality, still had resonance for this young British policeman."

The same experience happened to your author in 1971. At the Royal Institute of International Affairs, located at Chatham House in St. James Square, I was inquiring about some Murrow papers just a few days before returning to the United States. I told the young attendent on duty that I wanted to examine a speech by Ed Murrow. He pulled out a pen and leaned over the table to write.

"Ed," he said, and wrote out the name. "Murrow. How is that spelled, Sir?"

"M-u-r-r . . . "

"Oh, you mean Ed Murrow?" he comprehended.

"Yes," I said with some surprise. "How do you know of Ed Murrow?"

"Oh, I saw him on television, and on the BBC." he replied.

Occasionally, I would mention to Britons I met at bus stops or elsewhere what I was doing in England. In every case, there was recognition of the name, and usually a question about him, or simply a "Yes, I remember him." In the absence of any extensive permanent records of Murrow's wartime work, the memories about him that persisted more than a quarter century after he left England constituted a form of living memorial.

"Steady," a word frequently found in Murrow scripts, is the way Eric Sevareid saw Murrow's attitude toward the British. "This is what he loved about the British. Steady. They didn't panic, didn't get emotional. That quality seemed to mean a great deal to him. Be steady in your shoes." Even in his son Casey, Sevareid felt, this was what Murrow was looking for---a steadiness of character.

Adverse facts and statistics did not deter Ed Murrow's basic faith in the strength of the British people. His faith never wavered "when many people thought that maybe the British would go down. And I thought so at times," Sevareid admitted. "If they'd put out the RAF fighter force completely, what would have stopped them from invading? One by one they'd have sunk every naval vessel around the British Isles, and they'd have invaded." Once the enemy arrived in the British Isles, there would be nothing to resist them. As for Murrow's attitude, however, "He never believed it," said Sevareid. "Not for a minute. He knew somehow they'd come through this. And he was furious with people who took the defeatist line, even in private conversation."

But this view of the British was arrived at over a period of time, after many of the hard decisions of war had been made. Earlier, when he first arrived, Murrow did have some doubts, musings, and concerns about the British people, which he described in part in his touching farewell to the British people:

> I thought your streets narrow and mean; your tailors over-advertised; your climate unbearable; your class consciousness offensive. You couldn't cook; your young men seemed without vigor or purpose. I admired your history, doubted your future, and suspected that the historians had merely agreed upon a myth. But always there was something that escaped me.

At any rate, that was Ed Murrow's impression of the British when he first laid eyes on the island in 1930 as a visiting student. Nine years in England, however, changed him, as he noted in his eloquent tribute in 1946 when he said farewell to the British people whom he had come to love and respect. The phrases from that report, "A Reporter Remembers," clearly reveal Murrow's great devotion to the people and traditions of Britain:

> We all remember the spring of 1940 . . . and then how the grey German tide spread like a stain over Western Europe. There was Dunkirk---a name which will last so long as the English language.
> And there was Churchill who mobilized the language and made it fight.
> The big raid of December 29th when the city burned, and as I walked home at seven in the morning the windows in the West End were red with reflected fire, and the raindrops were like blood on the panes.
> That was the Christmas you sang carols in the shelters, and you were living a life, not an apology. And the defenders of the realm were the people who worked with their hands.
> And it was then that I learned the meaning of that great word "steady," in places like Bristol, Coventry,

> Plymouth, Southampton and Manchester.
> I believe that I have learned the most important thing that has happened in Britain during the last six years. . . . There was still law in the land, regardless of race, nationality or hatred. Representative government, equality before the law, survived.
>
> I have been privileged to see an entire people give the reply to tyranny that their history demanded of them.

Murrow was really a cosmopolitan and a teacher; his medium was simply somewhat different from most. Six years before delivering his famous "farewell," in the cold winter of 1940, Murrow had begun a new series on the BBC in which his job was essentially that of educating the British public about America. He did this by comparison, relating his home environment to his adopted one. Ringing through these programs was the dedication of a confirmed teacher, and the feeling of an internationalist who subscribed fully to the basic democratic principle that each person is important. There was, especially, a love of the British people that made it important to Murrow that he communicate effectively so that they would know about him and his kind back in America.

In this first 1940 broadcast, covering fourteen pages of script, Murrow outlined his own love of country, his sense of American history, and his devotion to its ideals of free speech, debate, and discussion. Throughout, he referred to the immigrant make-up of America and the fact that most if its inhabitants came from elsewhere, many from England and Europe: "Perhaps I should first of all present my credentials. I am English, Irish, French and German---an American as ever was---with ancestors who went out to the new world in the overcrowded ship called the Mayflower."

The series, according to Murrow, was aimed at informing the British about "the history of America . . . you'll hear something of our problems, the mistakes we have made, what we have done, or failed to do, about unemployment, conservation of natural resources; the Negro . . . ."

He began by comparing the size of America with that of Britain:

> Nine of the 48 states are larger than all of England, Scotland and Wales. I was in Texas and saw a sign in the southeast of the state: 'El Paso, 986 miles' and El Paso is in Texas too. The distance from London to Belgrade across one state.

Next he discussed the impact on America and Americans of the "British influence." It was they "who determined the character of its laws and institutions . . . with the English heritage of representative government came the English tradition or revolt against tyranny."

Throughout that first broadcast, Murrow used example after example to illustrate the mixture of backgrounds of those making up the country. On American history: "Our Declaration of Independence was signed by a Swede, three Irishmen, a Czech, four Scots, five Welshmen, five Scotch-Irish and thirty-eight Englishmen." On government: "The Chief Justice of the Supreme Court is the son of a Welshman. The Governor of Illinois is the son of a German immigrant. Our most popular songwriter is a Russian-Jewish immigrant." On language: "Whatever you think, the American language is basically English, but with words from all the nations whose people came to America." He gave an example: "Here is a sentence made up of Pennsylvania Dutch, Chinese, German, Irish, Italian and American: 'If a loafer has a yen for noodles, or ballyhoos spaghetti, he's okay.' That's American."

On cultural differences? Murrow suggested that there are many within the United States itself, to a point where some Americans would feel more at home in England than in other parts of their own country. "A New Englander from Boston will feel as much a stranger in New Orleans, with its French names, good food and damp, warm climate as he will in London. . . . Most Americans who live on either sea coast feel themselves in a foreign land when they are in the Southwest. . . . When English friends ask me: 'Why doesn't America do this or do that?' I am tempted to reply, 'Which America, which part of America, are you talking about?'"

Finally, he concluded: "Mine is a curious country. It is big, busy, and boisterous, full of contradictions---there is great wealth and dire poverty. We are a nation of many races and creeds---not easy to understand."

Ed Murrow knew his country, and he exerted much effort in trying to make it known to and understood by the British people, and *vice versa*. That speaks well for his concern and care for the people he lived with and came to know over nine years, for he seemed to go far beyond the call of duty in pursuing these objectives. But know them he did, in all their diversity, but he strove to reduce this diversity by overcoming the language "gulf" so as to increase understanding and cooperation between the two nations. Sir Winston Churchill once reflected on the "diversity" problem when he noted that the United States and England were "one nation divided by a common language." Sometimes the differences between the two peoples took some rather strange twists and turns. For example, while the British were ordinarily more formal and polite in their conversations, especially with strangers, the Americans tended toward familiarity and informality. Yet the roles could be exchanged, and, in the case of Ed Murrow, were to a considerable extent. Robert Reid emphasized this when he recalled, on a postwar visit to New York, how astonished he was to find everyone calling Ed "Mr. Murrow." Reid had first met him in 1942, and immediately found him "no prima donna. You automatically called him 'Ed.'"

Reid continued,

> I used to meet him quite often when he came to the North [referring to his native Yorkshire]. Now this is a very important point! Ed Murrow regularly used to come to

the North of England; there, people have a totally different philosophy of life. Some of us from the North say we're more sober; we're more industrious.

Ed sensed and knew the difference. He did not make the mistake the English do who go to America and regard New York and Washington as "the state of the country." Many Americans make the same kind of mistake by trying to equate England with London.

"Ed knew the 'typical' Londoner, and also those in the North," Reid elaborated further. "He knew the people who rode buses or the tube. He knew the sort of spirit the people had in those days. He knew the Cockney type, with their sharp wit. He knew the Scots and Welsh people."

Even in the North, Ed could detect differences:

He knew the difference between the Yorkshire and the Lancaster people. He knew there was a difference between the way people in the North and the South thought about things. He knew about the county rivalries between Yorkshire and Lancaster, going back to the War of the Roses.

It used to come out in odd little remarks he'd make in introducing you to somebody. 'This is Bob Reid, of the BBC. Of course he comes from the North of England. He's a Yorkshireman by birth, but he lived for a long time in Lancaster.'

When he and Murrow went back to Murrow's apartment after Reid had visited him at the "See It Now" studio in New York, Reid remembered returning to a rather palatial place on Park Avenue. On the way up in the express elevator, Murrow said, "It's only a poor place, but it's home."

"Now this is a typical British clack," observed Reid. "This is the sort of clack some of his more aristocratic or wealthy friends had said when they took him for a weekend in the country houses in the shires."

Reid even discerned a kind of understanding of the British in Murrow's body posture. One day Elmer Davis was brought over to meet officials at the BBC. Ed said little as Davis and the Director General, in the private office, talked about North Country dialect. Ed sat on his haunches, up against the wall. "I often wondered why he did that," said Reid, "and how many times he'd seen, on his travels through the mining district of the North of England, miners who traditionally sat on their haunches like that."

Richard Marriott summed it up best in attesting that of course Murrow loved the English and the rest of the British people: "He was a friend of Britain, no doubt about that. You don't stay in a place if you don't like the place, or remain in sympathy with it." Marriott felt that was true of any good correspondent. Murrow's record of nearly a decade of continuous service in Britain ought to prove adequate witness to this observation.

Yes, truly, Ed Murrow was a dedicated Anglophile and admitted it both in a straight forward way as well as in a thousand and one actions and mannerisms. What's more, he did much to help the British people to understand and better appreciate Americans and the United States as a nation. This mass production of mutual respect and even esteem was probably his biggest contribution to the war effort and to the ideal of continuing understanding between the two countries and their peoples.

CHAPTER XII

WARTIME SERVICE

Unquestionably, the wartime British public remembered Edward R. Murrow with fondness and thanks. But why the heartfelt appreciation? What was the service Murrow performed for Britain? Of what value was he to Britain? There is no dearth of theories that seek to explain this phenomenon. Although they are diverse, they focus on nuances of the same general theme: he was a true friend, indeed, to a friend in need---and he helped bring about the desperately needed assistance for that friend.

The *Daily Telegraph*, commenting in 1943 on a Sunday night program called "Postscript" on the BBC, put in a sentence: "His [Murrow's] talks from London since the war began, and especially during the blitz, have done enormous service in enabling Americans to understand our efforts and aims." In his lengthy history titled *The War of Words*, Asa Briggs credits the work of American correspondents---singling out Murrow, as usual---for the credibility of BBC news: "One main reason why the British account of what was happening was more acceptable at the time in the United States than the German account was the skill, the integrity and, above all, the courage of American commentators in London."

Murrow was one of the leaders who contributed effectively to counteracting the isolationist voices in the United States. Commented Briggs:

> The events of September and October 1940 spoke louder than words, particularly when they were interpreted in the stirring words, hot immediate words, of Ed Murrow and his fellow correspondents.

And the critical comments in American broadcasts "added to the sense of veracity." And Murrow was "always prepared, as Priestley was, to praise individual courage while criticizing social or political ineptitude." Briggs cited, as an example, Duff Cooper looking forward with great eagerness to more German bombers coming over, with Murrow observing that the Minister's time would be better spent in getting some of his dispatches through the censors in time to make the headlines of New York newspapers. And, Briggs further applauded: "As the 'blitz' continued, Murrow, brave, resourceful, superbly articulate, was always in the thick of it."

Erik Barnouw, in his history of American radio, put it quite directly. Ed Murrow, he felt, had impact, and he was very adept in the work of the professional persuader; probably consciously, but if not, still persuading all the same. Barnouw cited an example:

> As the Germans massed on the English Channel, Americans began to hear, night after night, a voice from London.

Murrow---calm, never arguing, never urging an opinion---
began to refer to himself as 'this reporter.' He narrated---and in so doing, had historic impact.

Barnouw concluded that the calm style of CBS news reporting during the war was successful in changing peoples' thinking while at the same time avoiding the appearance of trying to shape opinion. "If, however, CBS intended that opinion should not be shaped," stated Barnouw, "it surely failed. Murrow influenced many, and consciously or unconsciously must have wished to. It was not merely to transmit data that he haunted rooftops." By avoiding argument and overt persuasion, counterarguments were also avoided. However, "Murrow and his colleagues offered something akin to drama: vicarious experience of what they were living and observing. It put the listener in another man's shoes. No better way to influence opinion has ever been found."

After the war, Eric Sevareid in his memoirs addressed the question in his typically lucid flowing style:

> The generality of British people will probably never know what Murrow did for them in those days. A few in Whitehall and Fleet Street knew quite well, and their honoring of him was done not out of calculation, but out of simple gratitude for his understanding.

In Sevareid's view, Murrow was not trying to sell the British cause to America; rather, he was attempting to explain the universal human cause of men "who were showing a noble face to the world." In so doing, he humanized and universalized the British and their behavior, and his message was therefore compelling to his fellow countrymen.

"He was of far greater influence than the American ambassador to London," commented Sevareid. "He was the ambassador, in a double role, representing Britain in America as well as America in Britain." In chatting with many British wartime leaders it becomes quite apparent that, for many of them, Murrow was indeed more of an "ambassador" than the official United States Ambassador. "There is no doubt," wrote Sevareid, "of his immense aid to the President in awakening the American people to the issue before them."

Charles Collingwood essentially agreed with Sevareid that Murrow acted in the ambassadorial role of interpreter and representative: "Ed was a remarkable interpreter of the British to the Americans and equally so of the Americans to the British." And his was an enormous power, Collingwood stressed:

> He played this role which is larger than any broadcaster has played since. There's no broadcaster alive today who has this special role, who enjoys this special confidence that Ed did in one country, let alone in two countries.

Collingwood has also suggested a completely different additional contribution for which Murrow must be credited:

> He made radio news broadcasting respectable. No one knew what it was before. Ed made it respectable, and he did the same thing for television when we advanced into the television age. He made people realize that this was a serious effort.

At the time, many thought that whatever was on radio---and, later, television---must be frivolous by virtue of the essential frivolity of the medium. Ed's performance "was such that it was impossible not to take this medium seriously."

Not only did he make radio news responsible and create an image of a medium that must be regarded highly, Murrow also gave a boost to the credibility of the BBC. Asa Briggs, as already noted, thanked the American reporters for lending credence to the BBC accounts of events.

To Leonard Miall, this was Murrow's great service in the war of words. It was one thing for the Germans to say something, another for the British to say something. "On the other hand, if a neutral said something, and it happened to be the same as what the British were saying, it backed up the truth of the thing." As a result, the BBC constantly replayed programs by Murrow and others during the war period.

Specifically, Miall elaborated on the matter of atrocity propaganda. Throughout the war, he maintained, the BBC leaned over backwards to avoid what they called "growl propaganda" that had been done in World War I---stories of Germans melting down babies to make candles, and that sort of thing---and those working in information and propaganda services had grown quite cautious of atrocity propaganda. According to Miall, such propaganda "very soon boomerangs; you overexaggerate, and people begin to distrust anything you say about the enemy because it's all atrocity propaganda." When Buchenwald and Belsen were opened, the BBC had its own correspondents on the scene. Richard Dimbleby went into Belsen, was greatly shocked by what he saw, and broadcast it. But simply to report what actually was witnessed at these camps could sound so much like the old World War I atrocity propaganda, and thus not believable, that there was a genuine concern about the issue. But, for Miall, "One of the ways of gaining credibility, to show that this wasn't just atrocity propaganda, that these horrible things were happening, was to use Ed Murrow's broadcasts." The BBC of course rebroadcast Murrow's emotional and hard-hitting Buchenwald talk. The Corporation did so, says Miall,

> simply because Ed Murrow's reputation for telling the truth was so high that in a sense we trusted it, and we thought our audience would trust it, even above our own correspondents like Dimbleby.

It could have been easy for some audience members to think that the BBC was just "ladling it on;" that the BBC, in wanting to establish the total horror of the thing, had to lean over backwards to insure accuracy and credibility. "To let people eavesdrop on what Ed was reporting to the United States was, according to Miall, in a way, the most believable part of it."

Rightfully pointing out that to specify Murrow's most important contribution during the war assumes knowledge of all that Ed accomplished, Sir Lindsay Wellington still thought that there was one contribution which surpassed others---at least, others of which he might be aware:

> From *my* point of view his greatest contribution was his description of the British people at war, in all kinds of manifestations. It kept coming up. He kept going out on journeys through bombs with taxi drivers. He'd go to look at this. Go to look at that. To observe people at their jobs, talk to them.

Through his observations of the British, felt Sir Lindsay, Murrow was able to "boil all this up inside his head and bring it out in a series of broadcasts which I thought were of tremendous significance."

In spite of his comments about Murrow being a beneficiary of good timing and privileged only as other American commentators were, Thomas Barman felt that Murrow certainly was "useful" in one especially important sense. That sense, in agreement with Sir Lindsay, was in "bringing home to the American people what this country was taking by way of punishment; bringing home the virtues of the British people, if you'd like to put it like that." And the specific benefits emerging from that? "Certainly the sale of destroyers, lend-lease business. I think Ed Murrow and others contributed heavily to making that possible. Very heavily, indeed," commented Barman. Recognizing a certain charisma in Murrow, Barman pointed to Murrow's "American accent" as more masculine-sounding to the English ear: "He gave us the impression there was a friend standing by us, when there were precious few friends around." After all, Barman reminisced, the isolationist lobby during the early part of the war was a strong influence in America. In Murrow, "here was a friend at hand." Most observers agreed with Barman, many in almost the same words and phrases and certainly with equal enthusiasm, that "Murrow helped bring America into the war." And that was what England needed as a matter of survival.

Barman, when asked what Murrow was trying to accomplish, replied:

> He wanted the Americans to face up to their responsibilities. They either had to see the whole Western world go down with them, the United States go down with the Western world, or stand up and fight. It wasn't to save Britain or France. It was the whole Western world.

His historical analysis was that, up until 1914, America had been sheltered behind the British Navy. In 1939, that shelter was removed. "America had to be aroused to save itself."

Michael Balkwill summed it all up in a sentence: "The forming of American opinion on the issues of the war must be largely attributed to Murrow's reporting from London." But, emphasized Balkwill, it wasn't as false propaganda that this was accomplished. "Facts are better than propaganda. Murrow never reported in a way that directly stated: 'Aren't the British marvelous? We must join in their side.'" Because he reported specific scenes and stories, his influence was "profound." It would seem, however, that while Murrow shied away from direct appeal for aid to Britain, the net effect was to ask and, in effect, answer the implied question posed by Balkwill: "Aren't the British marvelous? We must join in their side."

Actually, Murrow was telling America that, in the sweep of events, "it could not escape involvement." This was the way Michael Standing put it: "He worked in a single-minded way to bring this home to America. He was himself a considerable influence in affecting American opinion as to participation in the war."

And Richard Marriott's response to the question of Murrow's wartime service to Britain noted that "He [Murrow] did an enormous amount to facilitate the United States' entry into the war." Colston Shepherd, a former BBC correspondent, has written that Murrow's diligent effort to check facts and "dig" for the news with his own personal observation was of inestimable value to the British.[1] Concluded Shepherd:

> In the long run his work did *us* as much good as it did *for* us in the United States. Neither the government nor British journalists influenced Ed's judgments and therefore his verdicts came near convincing us that we were better as a nation than perhaps we were.

At a time when the British people faced their greatest trial, such reassurances played a vital role.

A very gracious and charming hostess summed it all up, long after the war, one late afternoon over tea at the Royal Society for the Arts. She was a television producer who had worked with Murrow a few times on programs. She was also a biologist who had specialized in genetics in the 1920's before joining the BBC as talks producer on current affairs subjects. That charming hostess was Mary Adams, who smiled when asked to comment on Edward R. Murrow's contribution to the war effort, and said simply, "He believed in the cause. A moral conviction. A righteous cause. . . . Others wanted a good story."

---

[1] These and other comments that follow are based on a personal letter, dated April 8, 1971, written by Colston Shepherd to the author.

CHAPTER XIII

RECOGNITION

It was 1941, the war in Europe was more than two years old, and the shock for Americans produced by the Japanese attack on Pearl Harbor was only days away. At this fateful moment in history, Ed Murrow came home. He had left five years earlier, unknown and largely inexperienced. He returned weary, now experienced and recognized as a master reporter.

William S. Paley, CBS President, used the occasion of a testimonial dinner on December 2, 1941, honoring Murrow's return to enunciate CBS's policy of news freedom:

> Tonight we're celebrating both the survival of an ideal and a man's service to that ideal. I pledge you, as I have before, that Columbia will cherish it [freedom of the air] and fight for it no matter whence, nor how subtly or how boldly comes the attack.

Paley then introduced Murrow as "a man fitted to his time and to his task, a student, a philosopher, at heart a poet of mankind and, therefore, a greater reporter."

But it was poet Archibald MacLeish who saw a lofty and noble contribution that Murrow had made, one that involved more than an immediate wartime goal or the development of a new medium. For MacLeish, Murrow had been instrumental in altering the relationships among people: "You destroyed a superstition. . .the superstition which poetry and all the arts have fought for centuries . . . the superstition of distance and of time!"

How had he done so? MacLeish eloquently, and indeed poetically, spelled it out:

> You spoke, you said, in London. . . . But it was not in London really that you spoke. It was in the back kitchens and the front living rooms and the moving automobiles and the hot dog stands and the observation cars of another country that your voice was truly speaking. You made real and urgent and present to the men and women of those comfortable rooms, those safe enclosures, what these men and women had not known was present there, or real.

Never again would a nation of people be able to live in almost complete isolation. The new media of communication and men like Murrow had altered all that. He helped to unite people in a common cause by bringing the war directly to them through the sound of footsteps going to shelters, or bombs crashing down. To the realities and horror of war he added sympathy and sorrow, and a desire to help.

A quarter-century later, there came another war in far-off Vietnam. Again a medium---this time television---intruded into the back kitchens and the front living rooms in all its stark visualness, and the American people could, indeed, "See It Now." While Murrow had used the medium of radio during World War II to inform and to unify the American people, television, was used during the Vietnam war in such a way that millions of viewers began to question our involvement and purpose. The result was that the media helped to make the war unpopular, encouraged disunity by raising issues concerning America's moral position, and exposed to the world the helplessness of the world's greatest military machine in trying to cope with ragged guerrillas. There is every reason to believe that, had he lived through that era, Edward R. Murrow would have been in the forefront of those correspondents in the field intent upon bringing the truth to the American people regardless of its impact on the war effort. It was indeed a different time, a different war, and a different national purpose from the more clearcut, black/white, good/evil dichotomies that confronted Ed Murrow and his colleagues during that earlier war.

As for Murrow's role in 1941, several testimonials, which are more tributes than explanations, help to put his efforts into perspective. Sir Lindsay, for example, felt that "the occasion found the man. That is to say that his forcefulness---his directness and pungency of phrase---was particularly fitted to time of war." The man saw meaning in the occasion. That's what Robert Reid felt: "He had a great sense of occasion. It's all right to be a reporter. Facts, hard news, and how to organize them: that's the art of reporting." But for Reid there was something more, and that was Murrow's creative work: "You've got to have a sense of the occasion, the sense of history to see things in perspective . . . it was on a higher level. Ed had that more than he had the reporting."

Reid didn't intend, of course, to demean his reporting abilities:

> He was a good reporter, going out, getting the facts, and so on, but it was when he got down to describing a scene in London during a raid . . . you couldn't get any facts . . . but he gave those beautiful word pictures. . . . This is what he had.

Mary Adams, on the other hand, summed it all up very briefly: "He had a certain authoritarian decency."

In evaluating the contributions of this mass-media man of words, one is reminded of two other giants of the spoken word: Winston Churchill and Franklin Roosevelt.

Of all the places Americans visit in England, one of the most serene---a scene of great simplicity---is Churchill's private home at Chartwell in Kent. It is especially meaningful to walk slowly about the grounds and through the house in relative isolation on, say, a cold gray April day before the tourists begin to swarm over the grounds.

The sloping gardens, neatly trimmed hedges, the famous black swans, and Churchill's own brick wall---these suggest a kind of tranquil air where a nation's leader in time of peril could find self-renewal and strength. Inside the red brick house are spacious but always simply adorned rooms. It is a house that can today be "lived in," rather than being a museum or a "great leader's home."

The visitor perceives what he will. One might easily be struck by the quaint, natural pattern that typified almost every room. Others might be more fascinated by the fact that somewhere in each room was either a small or a large picture of Churchill's colleague, Franklin Roosevelt, or a letter to or from him.

It is evident that this display is not an attempt to cement Anglo-American relations. It is, rather, a reflection of genuine friendship between these two leaders, whatever history may say of their occasional disputes, disagreements, and political power plays. One instantly grasps, at Chartwell, that Roosevelt and Churchill---unconsciously, perhaps---embraced each other as closely related, mutually admiring human beings.

Both were men of words. Franklin Roosevelt, on this side of the Atlantic, stands alone as the political master of one medium. He is known, when his speaking is discussed, as the "Radio President." No man before or since had the ability, in that office, so to command the listener to pay rapt attention, to move his ear a little closer to the speaker, so as not to miss a word, to hear that baritone sonorously enunciate, "My fellow Americans . . . ."

Churchill's literary and spoken achievements are, of course, well documented and known. But it is Asa Briggs who notes that, while Churchill was truly a man of words, he apparently could not have cared less about broadcasting. In six volumes of Churchill's epic history, at any rate, there are less than ten references to the roles of broadcasting or the BBC. He never referred to his wartime broadcasts, or to the possible influence of broadcasting on the morale of the people or on wartime operations. Says Briggs,

> Unlike Hitler, who wrote in *Mein Kampf* that 'in wartime words are acts,' Churchill was always far less interested in persuasion and propaganda than in the conduct of military operations. . . . 'If words could kill, we would be dead already,' he told a radio audience in 1939.

Churchill may have minimized the role of broadcasting, but he was a superb practitioner of the art of spoken persuasion. As a British intelligence chief put it, notes Briggs, "When Churchill spoke or wrote a message it was always a deed, whereas when other ministers spoke it was often only words."

Churchill, in typical poetic metaphor, tossed his contribution aside: "The people's will was resolute and remorseless. I only expressed it. They had the lion's heart. I had the luck to be called upon to give and roar."

Edward R. Murrow sat and talked with Churchill many times. And in 1954, when Churchill turned eighty-four, Murrow went back to an earlier phrase ("he mobilized the language and made it fight") and embellished it only a little. He said of Britain's leader:

> He mobilized the English language and sent it into battle to steady his fellow countrymen and hearten those Europeans upon whom the long dark night of tyranny had descended.

Three men of words. Each knew the other personally. Each affected the course of civilization: two through government leadership and one through a different kind of leadership---among the peoples of the nations led by the other two.

What did Murrow accomplish in those early wartime years? Perhaps Franklin Roosevelt told him through a very simple act, when a nation was in shock, fearful and angry, at a time when every overwhelming burden crushed down like an avalanche on the President's back. At that moment, in the late midnight hours, Franklin Roosevelt ordered Ed Murrow to his private quarters for beer, sandwiches, and a long, cathartic talk.

The date was Sunday, December 7, 1941.

CHAPTER XIV

THE "OBJECTIVE" REPORTER

Facts. Accuracy. Truth. Integrity in reporting. Over and over, when one talks to those who knew Edward R. Murrow, or reads his scripts or examines articles, tributes, and books dealing with Murrow, these are the words that come ringing through. Somehow, in some way, Murrow achieved something more than others did in getting "facts, accuracy, and truth" into his reports, or at any rate, millions of people believed he did.

Did Murrow achieve, or even wish to achieve, that great ideal of journalism which is so talked about these days---"objectivity?" Was Murrow, in the last analysis, "objective" in handling Senator Joseph R. McCarthy? His "facts" were accurate, but there has been considerable controversy over Murrow's role. Was bringing into play the resources of a powerful broadcasting network a fair manner of handling the McCarthy episode, especially since the Senator in his "equal time" presentation blundered in an amateur way, with little of the time or resources needed for adequate preparation. Murrow himself was well aware of the power of the network. If it could dethrone a demagogue, like McCarthy, what could it do to a "good" man? And what about his reputation for objectivity in reporting during the war years? To evaluate the latter, we might move to the postwar period and examine Murrow's role in dealing with highly controversial subjects, a problem he rarely had to face in London.

Unquestionably, Murrow believed that emotion, the senses, the situation, and the feel of an event were also "facts," and part of the truth. Nevertheless, the question remains: Does "objective" reporting of the "facts" include, as "fact," the "feel" of an event?

As Walter Lippmann and others had noted back in the 1920's, just determining what is a "raw fact" is a difficult thing. What, for example, were the "raw facts" involved in what happened when thousands of people gathered together in the downtown area of Pittsburgh after the city's baseball team won a World Series? One "objective fact," of course, was that it was a celebration of happy people. Certainly that was true for most of the celebrants. On the other hand, if you were a store owner who had many dollars worth of property destroyed or stolen, it might have been better described as a riot involving looting. Moreover, were young ladies attacked or not? Did reporters actually observe all areas of the city? Many conflicting stories were reported by the media about those alleged events.

The "Pittsburgh event" and similar situations raise questions of objectivity in Ed Murrow's reporting. It would be impossible to analyze the reporting techniques of all others with whom he has been compared and contrasted. But we can examine and analyze his own views on the subject, and we can try to determine what others meant when they talked about his objectivity. We can also look at one or two of his reports to see what they reveal on this question.

As a mature reporter, Ed Murrow spelled out his views on the subject of "objectivity." He had spent nine years in London and had completed his reporting of the war; he had spent a year as a broadcast executive, and then had begun a series on daily radio news programs. He was not yet forty years of age; it was September, 1947.

He began that first American broadcast with a "personal word" about the series he planned to present, a series which was to run for twelve years. He began by quoting from a paragraph of his contract:

> News programs are broadcast solely for the purpose of enabling the listeners there to know facts---so far as they are ascertainable---and so to elucidate, illuminate and explain facts and situations as fairly as possible to enable the listener to weigh and judge for himself.

The goal of CBS News, as spelled out in the contract, was essentially to provide what the listener needed to weigh and judge developments for himself, but to "refrain---particularly with respect to all controversial, political, social and economic questions---from trying to make up the listener's mind for him."

According to his contract provisions, while the views of the news analyst should not intrude into a story, he had a responsibility to shed as much light as possible on the meaning of events as he saw and interpreted them. In performing this task, the news analyst should not say whether a particular occurrence was good or bad, and he should always endeavor to be fair in doing his job. He could, of course, present the opinions of various people or groups, when they were known and were relevant to a given issue, but he always would have the responsibility of providing "balances" in such presentations.

Murrow commented that the language of the contract was rather complicated, the "kind that lawyers like to write." He said that his own interpretation of its meaning was that his program was no place for personal opinion to be mixed up with ascertainable facts. Therefore, he would do his best to identify sources and to resist the temptation to use the microphone as a privileged platform. To this he added: "It is not, I think, humanly possible for any reporter to be completely objective, for we are all to some degree prisoners of our education, travel, reading---the sum total of our experience."

Thus Murrow publicly, on his national news program, stated his fundamental reportorial belief: objectivity is not entirely possible. Whether a novice or a well-trained and experienced reporter, the individual *could not be "completely objective."* He went on in his typically cautious manner to say that he would try to remember that "the mechanics of radio, which make it possible for an individual voice to be heard throughout the land, do not confer great wisdom or infallibility on that individual." Although he couldn't predict what would be covered on his news programs, he did rule out any "considerable amount of time devoted to news originating in divorce courts and maternity wards." Moreover, he recognized that he and his staff would make mistakes, but "the only thing that can be said about that in advance is that we shall do our utmost to be the first to correct them."

One area in which Ed Murrow was *not* objective was that relating to "fascism." To Murrow, this concept of totalitarianism, of the state over the individual, of government by authority and force, was not one which could be neatly balanced with "two sides to the question." Fascism was, is, and forever shall be morally wrong, and he never hesitated to say so. His travel, education, reading---the sum total of his experience convinced him to the very core of his being that fascism was an evil to be blotted from the face of the earth.

His views were shaped by his having seen too many weary expatriate German scientists and teachers in the 1930's, too many peoples subjugated, too much of Hitler and what he was doing to be "objective" about fascism.

In the war that he reported from 1939 to 1945, consequently, Ed Murrow was not objective, nor did anyone expect him to be. The fundamental premise of the democracies, with their similar traditions and histories, was opposition to fascism, and Murrow agreed completely with that premise. Out of this democratic tradition and his personal experience with fascism, Murrow reported what he regarded as "facts," and what others in the context of those times also regarded as "facts." In short, there was a virtual unity that did not strain the reporter in World War II as it would later in Vietnam. A unified country, fighting with all its resources against a deadly evil, provided a context of truth and accuracy that the milieu of a divided nation in a war in a remote corner of the world did not. For the public, the one had a ring of credibility because the public wanted to believe the news they heard, especially the news of advances, of victories won. The other war was characterized by mass skepticism, especially of official reports and the statements made by the nation's leaders.

Richard Marriott was blunt and to the point, therefore, when he said, "I think Ed had a general line [in his World War II reporting], really. How do you become objective about fascism? You can be objective about the Common Market, devaluation, if you're a reporter, but can you in a time of an overwhelming war situation?"

Eric Sevareid has recalled coming back to the States in 1940 following the fall of France and after a short stay in Britain working with Murrow. He said he had not realized the effect that Murrow was having back home:

> It suddenly hit me when I got there. . . . He made no pretense about being neutral or objective. You know, we were a neutral country. As a reporter, his heart and soul was 'cause.' Made no bones about it. Convinced we'd have to be in the war.

As Charles Collingwood saw it, "During the war broadcasts and later during the 'Hear It Now' and 'See It Now' things, there always was a subjective thing [about his work], but Ed was quite aware of this." He tried always to discourage subjectivity in himself because he believed that objectivity should be the ideal, that the job of a broadcaster was to inform rather than to persuade.

According to Collingwood, Murrow knew that in the process of informing, the individual's attitudes always colored the story in some way. In effect, his theory seemed to be that if you included all aspects of an issue or case, and if your own preferences leaked through, well, so be it.

And, according to Collingwood, Murrow believed in specific personal comment or personal editorializing,

> but he always insisted that it be *labeled* his opinion. If he gave his opinion, he would say so. Or he would say, 'Here I am going into . . . personal . . . opinion.' The opinion part was always separated from the informative part, and specifically labeled so. In other words, there was nothing sneaky about the way he got his opinion through.

In a personal interview, the author inquired of Collingwood: "What about this business of seeing two aspects of the story in reference to the war?" Fascism was one thing, sure. But German people were getting hurt as well. What about their suffering? Collingwood responded in this way:

> Well, he was the most humane of men. I think he did see; as I remember it, he had nothing but contempt for the policy of laying waste to Germany after the war, of making a Carthage, a Carthaginian settlement of Germany; he'd known Germans in his days of student organization work.
> I don't think he had any racial feeling for them, but you may be right, he may have been tempted to lump all Germans with the paranoic gang around Hitler.
> I don't suppose he thought greatly, or suffered greatly, at the undoubted pain that was being inflicted on the German people. No . . . nor I suppose did very many others in England at the time. Robin Duff, in Scotland, told me that 'Ed was the least objective of reporters. He was the crusader, more a statesman than a reporter.'

Thomas Barman, in his jovial but directly pointed manner, asked,

> What else were his broadcasts designed to do but stimulate American public opinion on the side of the British Isles? He must have had that in mind. . . . He couldn't possibly be objective. He would have been terribly stupid, which Ed Murrow was not, if he thought his broadcasts were just explanatory stories, told over the air.

Two others, however, were a little more analytical in probing the question of Ed Murrow and his objectivity in his broadcasts. When it came to the facts in a story, Murrow was "utterly concerned with objectivity," according to Michael Standing:

> He was very careful indeed to check his facts. But I think he overlaid this---not improperly, but very properly---with his own total conviction that these facts had implications which simply had to be seen on the other side of the Atlantic.

Standing claimed that Murrow certainly never misrepresented facts, but would comment upon them in a way that accorded with his own beliefs: "He applied himself to putting a lot of us right about woolly thinking over issues that were basically important." Standing stressed that Murrow had a rare talent for perceiving the truly significant:

> I think he had that editorial capacity, which is granted to not very many people, to single out the really salient factors in a position and to discard, especially in reporting, what was trivial and unimportant although spectacular in appearance.

In short, he was able to see through "frothy kinds of controversy."

Godfrey Talbot expressed somewhat the same view in a slightly different way: "Oh, he was a personal reporter all right, but he didn't allow personality to intrude, get in the way of the facts, or distort or color or influence the objectivity, the true picture or true story." It was because he was a sensitive person who felt things deeply that he was a good broadcaster, Talbot noted. He responded to events and people. And his broadcasts? "Of course they were personal. He was objective *and* personal. His broadcasts of the scenes were real, because this was a real, full human being who had experienced them, giving his own reactions to them." According to Talbot, all reporting is personal because it is all involved with the personal reactions of the reporter. It passes through the mind, out the mouth, and into the microphone. And Murrow was

> obviously a human being; credible, of course authoritative. You believed that he knew what he was talking about. But he was the very antithesis of the pundit on a pedestal giving, with a fanfare of trumpets, the great nine o'clock broadcast.

In discussing the question of objectivity with Eric Sevareid, I reminded him that in England, most of those who worked with Murrow during the war had kept emphasizing his concern for "facts, accuracy, and truth." After all, I suggested, news is objective. Sevareid replied:

Oh, not entirely. He was not. I was, at the start, much more inclined to be neutral-minded and objective; partly, I trained as a journalist. In college, on newspapers, as a very young man. Age of 17 or 18. Ed never was [trained as a journalist].

He just had this gift, you know, this great gift, you know, this great gift for getting at the heart of things. He was a great journalist. It was always just in him.

When the war came along, this was Good and Evil as far as he was concerned. A lot of preacher in Ed, you know.

Sevareid mentioned that all the American reporters got that way as time passed and the "crunch" came, especially when the United States got into the war.

"But this instinct for drawing back a little, being a little objective, what not . . . he didn't have much of that from the beginning. Wasn't in his training. Maybe that was one of his great strengths." Sevareid may have put his finger on it in saying that Murrow was perhaps not really capable of "drawing back a little" and, rather, reported as much as possible of the "feel and meaning" as he felt and interpreted an event.

Here we might briefly examine portions of a couple of scripts. Two on file in the BBC Archives can illustrate a Murrow report and how he involved himself with the story. Reference has already been made to the emotion that Murrow felt after Buchenwald. That broadcast, in its first-person narration, was vivid although necessarily selective in detailing facts. He saw the worst kind of human degradation, death, and suffering, and he reported what he saw along with his feelings.

In the introduction to that script, however, he said, "In the large cities [of Germany] there are many young men of military age in civilian clothes." One could ask a variety of questions concerning the meaning or intent of such a remark. First of all, one might wonder how many are "many," and does the reporter have a mandate to specify just how many? Did he observe any young men in civilian clothes in England, or anywhere other than Germany? Did he "see" more such young men in Germany than elsewhere? Yet, did not Hitler use even children---some not in their teens---in the final desperate hours of the Third Reich? If so, why did Ed Murrow see "many young men in civilian clothes?" Was he implying that young men were trying to hide their identity? That they had evaded service? That they did not want to be caught, or were being cowardly? We don't know. There is no further elaboration of that observation.

The point is, images were created, producing "pictures in the heads" of Murrow's listening audience. Perhaps his presentation should have spelled out what he had observed in more detail. He also showed a modicum of sympathy in references to "old men and women at work in the fields," and concluded that some German cities were so leveled by bombing as to "make Coventry and Plymouth appear to be merely damage done by a petulant child." On the other hand, he noted that the Germans "are well clothed, appear well fed and healthy, in better condition than any other people I have seen in Europe." Is this too strong a generalization? Had he seen enough of Germany in just a few days to make such a comparison with other countries in Europe? Logically, why would the Germans be so well fed, healthy, and cared for if indeed their cities were so leveled that "Coventry and Plymouth" suffered merely the damage of petulant children? Obviously, all countries---including Germany---suffered in wartime, and the inhumanity of war affected millions of victims on both sides.

Murrow was not thinking of "Germans in general" and their suffering when he saw Buchenwald. Nor would anyone have expected him to do so. Questions, such as those posed above, were simply not---in the context of the general truth of the times---questions to be asked or worried about. The truth was that the Germans, in everyone's mind, were *the* enemy, and Buchenwald only underscored that "fact."

The point is that personal values were clearly exposed in this broadcast. Can personal values ever be completely divorced from an analysis of events or observation of "facts," in covering the news? That basic question remains essentially unanswered.

But let's look at a less dramatic broadcast. Earlier in the war, in October of 1942, Murrow reported on the battle for El Alamein in Africa, and on new bombings in Italy. There was his story about General Montgomery: "He doesn't smoke or drink, and is about as close to a Prussian disciplinarian as you'll find in the British Army." There were two other stories of note in that broadcast, along with more trivial items. Russia and England were disagreeing about a trial for Rudolf Hess, and Mrs. Roosevelt was coming to England.

Here, in part, is how Murrow handled these stories. The italics are the *author's observations* (are they objective?) of Murrow's inclusion or intrusion of himself into the stories or areas where more specific detail and information are needed:

> The only agitation for a Hess trial in this country is coming from the Communist Party, and their argument too is that a gesture is needed. But *most people seem* [how many are "most"? Did he talk to "most" people?] a little tired of gestures, and more interested in action. And the action that's demanded and expected is not trials [*who says*?]. Hess is being treated as a prisoner of war, and Russian prodding will not cause him to be tried before the end of the war. *Perhaps* the attitude might be different if British cities were being heavily bombed, *but I doubt it*. There were *a great many people* in this country [again, *how many* is a *great many*?] who feared that Russia might be too successful in this war.
>
> They were afraid that the Continent of Europe might go Communist, and that it might spread to this country. *Maybe* there are still *a few* people who worry about that; but *it is lunacy* [*who says*?] to suggest that the second front is being held up for political reasons, or that

the British are holding Hess in reserve in order to make some kind of deal with the Germans. *Some strange things may happen before this war is over, but not that.* [Maybe so, but any indication of *why*? Or why the *strength* of Murrow's view? The best opinion here seems to be "all right, maybe he can't reveal his sources," but a general qualification about *who* represents the best opinion should be included.]
It seems to me that the majority of people have come to think . . .

In the last line, Murrow is very clearly saying, "Well, rather than a general truth, this is one person---me---evaluating opinion here." Is this evident in other sections? Of Mrs. Roosevelt's visit, he said:

One trouble about very distinguished visitors to this country---or to any other country for that matter---is that *they are likely to spend all their time in official company, and fail to understand that there are attitudes and forces at work which may not be reflected by High Government officials.* [Prejudgment? Why not observe that some visitors don't meet the people and *say, directly, that he feels that they should*?]
It's not easy to understand much about a country at war in two and a half weeks, but if energy, curiosity and good humor can do it, Mrs. Roosevelt will understand a lot about this country by the time she leaves.
I hope that someone, perhaps several people, *will be frank enough to tell Mrs. Roosevelt that we are doing pitifully little to make the United States understood in this country* at a time when the British people have more curiosity than ever before about America and things American.

In the fall of 1942, Murrow reported on the American elections. In reading the script, one can't help wondering whether the British government---or Murrow---was unhappy with the results of the elections:

The news from America about the American elections has affected some members of the government like a cold draft on the back of the neck . . . .
The thing that shook *certain people* [?] over here was a memory. . . . *They* [?] have no questions about the vigorous conduct of the war, but *they* [?] are wondering what the political trend means for the postwar world. . . . There are *those in responsible positions* [such as?] who wonder whether history may repeat itself . . . .

Was the omission of identification of "they" a matter of security? Of protection of sources? On what basis did a Republican victory become evidence in Britain that real concern about the postwar world was developing? Perhaps it was, but the explanation is simply not there.

A year later, Murrow speculated that perhaps the British were growing weary of the war: "They are getting irritable . . . I think it's probably caused by fatigue." He suggested that perhaps with the first sight of victory came a subconscious realization that problems would press in on the country after the war.

But this broadcast contained a direct comment by him that this was mere conjecture on his part. Was this an admission that he might be wrong? "Of course, it may be that this change in temper exists only in my imagination. I've spent most of the last four months in North Africa and in America." He had asked his wife, Janet, about the question, and she concurred that people were indeed tired.

Certainly the latter comments were objective in the sense that he was indicating a personal reaction, and conceding that it might be in error. The former example needed at least further evidence to support his contention about the effect of American elections. Why would one off-year election in America be fraught with such postwar implications? If he couldn't identify leaders, could he have elaborated on their arguments? Or were Murrow's feelings intervening without our knowing it?

That, it seems is the question. We just don't know. On another occasion, Murrow reported that some responsible people foresaw an end to the war in 1943: "That is their opinion. . . . I report it without sharing it."

For each instance presented here from his newscasts, other items and arguments can be found that come out clearly, thoroughly, analytically backed by carefully enunciated assumptions and theories, with key sources identified. A highly subjective but firmly grounded analysis of the problems of peace and planning for it may be found in his 1943 broadcast, referred to above. In several pages, he discussed the military and political implications of planning for a peacetime world based on history, opinions expressed at the time, and complaints and criticisms raised. So he concluded,

> Talking with people in this country, reading reams of Axis broadcasts, listening to tales brought here from the occupied countries, one cannot escape the conclusion that our affairs would be much advanced by some statements about what is to happen after unconditional surrender.

But let's leap forward a few years, to Murrow and television---and objectivity. One broadcast in a political campaign should suffice as a cogent example. It was a "See It Now" report, in which one of the features was a report on the prospects of Senator Robert Taft, who was campaigning for the Republican nomination for President in 1952. Geoffrey Bridson, former BBC writer and producer, was in the studio watching that telecast, and he talked with Murrow about it afterward. His story is a most interesting and relevant one bearing on the question of objectivity. His theory about what happened is instructive.

Bridson had been in New Orleans when Taft was there. A camera team had been sent to cover Taft's campaign through the South. The idea was to get filmed impressions of one candidate's campaign. "Ed was not a great believer in Taft, I gather," Bridson said on the basis of what happened.

Bridson pointed out that in going from city to city---from Birmingham to Memphis and from Memphis to Atlanta and elsewhere---a candidate will tend to repeat himself. Each audience is different, but a routine develops. "So Ed did a very naughty thing." With a full-throated laugh at the end of the telling, Bridson described the editing of the film:

> Ed filmed the same sort of thing in each town, particularly the fund-raising dinner where you sat down to a 100-dollar plate, with shots of people hacking away at their steaks and eating as fast as they could, and there was a singing chorus behind Taft as he came up, singing all the jingles. It was quite amusing the first time.
> Infinitely more amusing after you had left Memphis and gone on to Atlanta and the same thing happened. On to New Orleans, and the same thing happened there.
> Of course it was hilariously funny to watch. It was perfectly objective reporting.

But just rapid intercutting of people eating the same meal, singing jingles one after another, and the candidate---that wasn't the end of the story:

> What was funnier still was, before this came on, there were two or three other items, one from Korea and the other from Europe. Right at the beginning, as sort of a teaser to the show, Ed went over to Taft who was sitting at home in his living room waiting for the show to begin.
> Ed spoke to him: 'Well, Senator, we'll be joining you later in the show, after you've had a chance to see the film we made of your campaign in the South.'
> As I recall, Taft replied, 'Yes, Ed, I'm much looking forward to that.'
> So the show went on; then, this film was shown. It was so funny, I was trying to imagine what Taft was feeling while watching the film. Anyhow, at the end of the film Ed said, 'Well, we will now go over to the Senator to see what he made of that.'
> When the Senator came on screen, he had a slightly sickly but very creditable smile, and said, 'Well, Ed, I thought that was very fair.'

But after the show was over, Bridson talked to Murrow and learned something else:

>I said, "My God, I never saw anybody pull a gag like that before."
>Murrow said, "Brother, you saw nothing. I was watching Taft on my monitor while he was watching the film. You should have seen him then!"
>Taft was sort of boiling with rage, knowing at any moment he would have to appear, and appear not to be rattled---because he couldn't afford to be frightfully angry, because it would have spoiled his image.

Two decades ago, in the infancy of the use of television as a political force, perhaps such an incident was simply a small one, of little consequence, and, as Bridson indicated, just a jolly good joke. In the modern context of "poli-television'---with all that implies about hard sells, soft sells, set-ups, stagings, and commercial marketing techniques applied to candidates, not to mention the problem of "fairness,"---the incident appears less funny. In fact it gives every evidence of a total lack of objectivity in the reporting of the Taft campaign.

But Bridson felt that "this was being just rather naughty and extremely funny. Quite obviously, it didn't do Taft any harm at all. You don't lose a million votes by a picture of someone cutting a piece of steak on a plate."

It was just a gentle poking of fun in the same sense that a cartoonist in a newspaper pokes fun, Bridson felt; and the question of objectivity applied to newspapers "is never raised. Every newspaper is slanted one way." Bridson furthermore looked at the objectivity question as "something which on occasion one must dispense with."

He felt that *choice* in news reports was the important thing:

>In a country like America where you have so much radio and television to choose from, I don't think there is the same necessity there, possibly, to be absolutely middle-of-the-road objective. What you lose on the CBS roundabout, you pick up on the NBC swings. The whole thing balances out.

The "balancing" process occurred not just between separate networks, Bridson felt, but "within any good broadcasting service." He used his own experience as an example:

>At the BBC, I used to be objective if I thought objectivity was called for; on the other hand, if I was writing about some controversial subject in which a great deal was said on both sides of the question I decided at the beginning, as a writer, that if you try to see both sides of any question, you are dead as a writer.
>Over the course of twenty-four hours, let alone months, a responsible broadcasting organization will lean to one side, then will lean to another side. But

if everybody is sort of walking a tightrope down the dead center, you have no listeners, no viewers; it's so dull!

I'm glad to see, every time I open a newspaper, there are howls of pain from the conservatives, who say the BBC is absolutely full of rabid Reds; and I know, perfectly well, a week later there will be shrieks from the other side that it's a hive of Tory activity. You know, this is the best test of an organization. We are there to use our intelligence. It all balances out.

Bridson is an experienced writer, and many of his programs---as outlined in his book *Prospero and Ariel: The Rise and Fall of Radio*[1] (a personal history of his work with the BBC)---are dramatic, artistic efforts based on his wide literary background. When asked if what he was describing could be applied to news writing, not just the personal artist's special program for radio. Bridson answered:

Yes, of course! Anybody who watched Ed knew perfectly well what his standpoint was. If they flatly disagreed with Ed, regarded him as a dangerous radical, they probably didn't watch him, or if they did, with the brakes on so much they'd automatically discount anything that he said.

His views were those of any Western liberal. He was in the great liberal tradition which, after all, was responsible for the foundation of the United States. I don't really see why you should object to liberalism. [Laughter.] Liberalism has a long tradition, and Ed is in that tradition.

The author as interviewer then attempted to sum up Bridson's ideas, to be certain his message would be accurately reported:

Smith: You're saying that any individual person in the medium with integrity, who isn't obviously falsifying facts, should definitely, in the liberal tradition, speak his mind, get involved, take a point of view. But in the responsible organization in which he works, these things in the long run will balance out with different personnel involved?

Bridson: CBS wouldn't have employed Ed Murrow in the first place if they didn't think he was a man of integrity. You don't go around looking for a screwball, giving him a platform---saying, "All right now, Brother, bring on Red revolution." Of course you don't. You don't if you have doubts of his integrity.

---

[1] D. G. Bridson, *Prospero and Ariel---The Rise and Fall of Radio; A Personal Recollection* (London: Victor Gollancy Ltd., 1971).

> Ed's integrity was as good as you could get. He knew what he was talking about. He knew the audience he was appealing to. They knew him. This was a love affair between the artist and his public.

In the discussion, Bridson repeatedly referred to Murrow as

> a man of integrity: a man who had strong feelings about certain things which he believed in, things which he believed to be right and true and just. When those things were at issue, I think Ed probably, mercifully, sort of left his objectivity behind.

After all, he continued, the BBC was certainly committed to an objective, fair, and thorough news organization. Bridson said that the Director General, Carleton Greene, once told him that the BBC was objective "except where the fundamental truths of life were concerned. They did not propose ever to be objective about injustice, intolerance, prejudice or anything like that. That was where objectivity was wrong. I think that was also the case with Ed."

Reducing the question of objectivity to absurdity, Bridson said that if a reporter on the scene were describing the decapitation of Charles I in a completely objective fashion, it would not only be a bad broadcast, but "a curiosity, eccentric."

Then Bridson put down his coffee cup in the Savile Club, to which Murrow himself had belonged. Pausing a moment, he summed up his entire discussion of objectivity, based on his many years as a writer, producer, and interviewer for the BBC.

"Any man I've admired in this business has decided what he thinks is right, and then gone ahead and said it. Whether Ed---or I---was ever right, who is to decide?"

With that enigmatic query, we shall leave the issue of "the 'objective' reporter" to the subjective judgment of our readers. That is probably the way Ed Murrow would have wanted it.

CHAPTER XV

UNHAPPY EXECUTIVE

  Twice in his career---once at the mid-point, again at the end---Edward R. Murrow held high-level executive posts. After his broadcast experience in wartime London, he came back to New York as a CBS executive vice-president. In 1961, he went to Washington as Director of the United States Information Agency (USIA) under President John F. Kennedy. He had, of course, served as executive head of the Columbia Broadcasting System in London, but that was a minor executive post, with the major portion of his time devoted to broadcasting. Still, as a head of a small corps of reporters, he had acted in the capacity of administrator, and that role might be added to his two major appointments.
  Some aspects of his work as an administrator have already been described. Now it's time for evaluation. Did the "Peter Principle" apply in Murrow's case---i.e., was he promoted to administrative positions that enabled him to reach the highest level of incompetency? If the Peter Principle applied only to attitude, the answer would have to be a firm, yes! No matter what the source, all available evidence indicates that Murrow simply did not like the role of administrator. But enjoy it or not, was he nevertheless a capable one? Measured comparatively with other administrators, perhaps he was not the overwhelming success that he was as a reporter. But by no means did he fail, and there is some indication that he breathed a new spirit into the USIA---not terribly surprising, in view of his personal dedication.
  Still, the record does not show quite the enthusiastic endorsement here that Murrow achieved in other aspects of his work. The best way to evaluate Murrow as an administrator is to seek knowledge and evaluation of that role from those who worked for him. What did they think of the boss? Who would know Murrow's functioning as an administrator better than those who had observed him and worked with him under his supervision daily as he carried out that role under the trying conditions of wartime broadcasting?
  Charles Collingwood and Eric Sevareid have offered their impressions on this subject. Romney Wheeler, who worked for Murrow when he was directing the USIA, was also willing to offer his views on Murrow's later role as an administrator. Our conclusions on Murrow's administrative abilities will be based on the first hand experiences of these three outstanding individuals.
  One positive quality Murrow had as an executive was his ability to hire capable staff. It is both an understatement and a compliment merely to point out the small army of reporters still active and outstanding today who first came into CBS via Murrow's door.

But if hiring capable people was a Murrow talent, firing was not. That, at any rate, was the way both Sevareid and Collingwood saw it.

Collingwood recalls that Eric Sevareid and Larry LeSeur were hired before he was, as well as Bill Shirer, who was in Berlin. Collingwood's career closely paralleled that of Howard K. Smith. Smith had been at Oxford with him, and both had been hired on the same day to work for United Press. Both covered the Ministry of Information. Smith went to Berlin and, after Shirer had to leave Berlin, remained as a kind of "stringer" for CBS while working full time for United Press.

"Then," said Collingwood, "in the fullness of time, Ed or Paul White offered Smith a permanent job, so he worked for us in Germany and then had to spend most of the war in Switzerland when he got out." Smith has, of course, had a long and distinguished career in television news, and is currently with the ABC evening news.

Russia constituted a special problem as far as news gathering and reporting were concerned. Collingwood said it was a problem getting correspondents into the country because of the very strict Russian censorship. All correspondents there were under surveillance, and very little hard news came out except for the officially approved Soviet communiques during the war.

Commented Collingwood:

> I can remember saying to him [Murrow], 'I would think what you ought to do about Russia is to get a very good feature writer, someone to tell the anecdotes, give the flavor of life in wartime Russia, rather than just paraphrase the communiques.'

Murrow bought the idea, and Collingwood introduced him to still another United Press colleague (U.P. appears to have been a basic training school for broadcast journalists), Bill Downs. "Bill equipped himself with an enormous great sheepskin-lined coat and went off to Russia, where he did a marvelous job."

Collingwood stressed that in such matters Murrow was very much in charge; but the two were close friends, and consultations and informal talks about matters of hiring took place regularly. It was Murrow, however, who had, and used, the authority to make final decisions.

Sevareid described it in his book of many years ago, and he still remembers the debt he owed Murrow for his job: "Oh, he hired me. But somebody else would have fired me along the way if it hadn't been for Ed."

It was Sevareid's feeling that he was, as he put it, "a lousy speaker." He continued:

> But there was enough impact from some of my scoops, and some of my writing . . . that sort of saved me, and Ed respected that.
>
> I think he admired my writing, and some of my reporting in France and England I think he was very excited about.

> I think I was a strain on him a good deal. But nevertheless, he saw clearly what qualities I did have, so he hung it out all right. Stayed with me.

In Collingwood's words, "Ed couldn't bear to fire anybody." And according to Sevareid, "He hated to decide what they'd be paid, or to fire them. . . . He couldn't stand that."

Collingwood said that Murrow discovered, when he became an executive, that he was not a very good administrator. When asked whether the problem was that he was not good at it, or that he just didn't like to be an administrator, the answer was,

> Well, as a matter of fact, I think he was pretty good. He didn't like it, because being a good administrator inevitably means that sometimes you have to be hard on people; individuals have to suffer . . . can't give the pay raise you'd like to. . . . He went through hell when he presided over the separation between CBS and Bill Shirer, who was his great friend.

Regarding another colleague, Sevareid said, "He fired Paul White [who was] the first great managing editor of broadcast news." It was a regrettable story that Sevareid related:

> When Ed became Vice-President after the war, he jumped over White. White was a hard drinker. And White one day had to do a broadcast, introducing Bob Trout when they started this series. An evening radio thing Ed later took over.
> White was so frightened at being on the air, himself, that he just got drunk. And he sounded drunk on the air. And Ed was listening upstairs, at 485 Madison, and . . . I wasn't there, but I'm told that he came down in a white rage, and he fired Paul White on the spot.
> The guy had a great reputation, helped build us.

Paul White went to San Diego, where he taught and wrote a book on broadcast news. Murrow may have fired White, but apparently he never forgot White's talents. In a short note I received from Murrow in 1955, he advised me---a young army sergeant at the time---how to get into broadcast news. The letter strongly recommended a book entitled *News on the Air*. It was written by Paul White.

Other comments by Collingwood and Sevareid regarding Murrow's role as an administrator are more clearly differentiated. Sevareid was blunt and direct. He contended that Murrow demanded little of his wartime staff: "Damn little. He hired people that he thought knew what to do, and left them on their own. He was a lousy administrator."

Collingwood, however, reflected that Murrow, in his capacity of running a small bureau or small organization, "was very good, because he had the wonderful ability of delegating authority. Instead of leaning over other people's shoulders, he would make assignments and expect people to perform them well." But Murrow never kept pressure on, never used constant prodding or pushing.

According to Collingwood, "If somebody fell down on an assignment, Ed would let it be known he was unhappy. And since the people who worked with him had the most unstinting loyalty to him, the thing they most wanted to avoid was to make him unhappy." It wasn't a matter of his staff being afraid of his wrath, but rather trying to avoid the feeling that they had let him down.

"The result was that he always got the very best out of the people who worked for him---and with him---that they could give. This is a quality of leadership, I think." Collingwood emphasized that Murrow would never back down on a matter of principle. He was referring not only to the McCarthy broadcasts, but to his relations with the parent company, CBS, as well.

"I know there were times when he and Paul White in New York didn't see eye to eye on how a story should be covered, or what should be covered, or the selection of some story . . . that kind of thing." However, added Collingwood, Murrow had enough "ascendancy" in the hierarchy to prevail.

He was also capable of compromise, Collingwood concluded:

> He wasn't bullheaded. If there was something Paul White wanted or someone else wanted particularly, even though his own judgment was that better things might be done with the time, he'd go along with it. I don't want you to get the impression he was abrasive. . . . He was not abrasive. On the other hand, he was not at all an easy man to push around.

Sevareid recalled two incidents which revealed Murrow's emotions and feelings in administrative situations. One involved a broadcast with Sevareid and Hans Von Kaltenborn. Sevareid confesses that he was "scared to death" over his first broadcast from London. Each speaker had only a given amount of time. "Kaltenborn, who was there, began to ad-lib, and I was to follow him." Kaltenborn talked on and on, and Sevareid ended up with only a minute to compress his copy; he felt that "instant editing" his part of the broadcast was a disaster and totally ruined it. "It fouled me up, made me nervous. I had to cut as I read. Ed just darkened with rage. Maybe at me, but mostly at Kaltenborn." Immediately after the broadcast, they walked to the elevator, Murrow not saying a word, just marching on ahead of the two of them. He crushed a pencil in his hand, breaking it in two. He was obviously furious, but he didn't say a word.

"He could lose his temper very quickly, though he would hold it in. I always knew, though." But his anger passed, apparently, as readily as it came. Added Sevareid:

> He had those rages, but then he'd sometimes be sorry and he'd apologize very indirectly, not directly. You know, he'd chew you out terribly one day. Next day, he'd call you up and ask your advice about something. That was his way of apologizing.

The second incident that involved Sevareid occurred on the occasion when Murrow left as Vice-President of CBS, to return to broadcasting. He had been an executive for about a year after the war, and he had sent Sevareid to Washington to run the CBS bureau there. Sevareid explained: "I was terrible at it, and didn't want to do it. But because he asked me, I did. I wanted to come here, but I didn't want to run the bureau." Sevareid agreed to do it because Murrow "was up there [in New York], to backstop everybody." But then he read in *Variety* that Murrow had given up his executive post to take over the 6:45 radio news that Bob Trout had had a ten-year contract to do. "This is what Ed should have been doing all the time," Sevareid emphasized. "You don't take the greatest broadcaster on earth and make him an executive. That's crazy."

As soon as Sevareid read the *Variety* story, he called Murrow. Was it true that he was leaving the job? In recalling the incident, Sevareid held his arms out in a gesture of futility, and, with a vocal emphasis that indicated the incident could have taken place yesterday, he said: "I didn't know what to say. I was broken up. Almost sat there and wept. He hadn't told me! No warning of this! He didn't tell anybody!"

Murrow asked Sevareid to come up to New York where, as Sevareid described it,

> We sat around, sort of looking at one another, not saying much. Having a drink. And, finally, he said something like 'Well, sorry you had to read about it in the papers. I should have told you . . . .'"

Sevareid said it was obvious that Murrow knew how upsetting the whole incident had been to him: "He felt as though he hadn't quite come clean with us. But I think it all happened too fast." He felt bad about it and obviously guilty. "You could always tell when he'd feel guilty about something. He wouldn't bull it through, but he'd make it up some way."

Sevareid had been hurt, and he had the feeling of being stranded after taking on a job he hadn't wanted only because his good friend and colleague had urged him to do so. Sevareid had agreed, assuming support from the executive front up north. In remembering the experience years later, Sevareid lowered his voice and spoke slowly as he gazed out the window of his Washington office: "He was a difficult man. A strange man in many ways. But he was the most extraordinarily exciting man I ever worked with or knew, I think." He added that many of his colleagues were greatly indebted to Murrow. "He just made our whole professional lives for us."

Reference was made, at the introduction of this discussion, to Murrow's reputation for breathing new life into the United States Information Agency. And so he may have done. But that is another subject, itself worthy of researching. One other comment is included here, however, because it bears on Murrow's work as an administrator. Whatever he accomplished in Washington after the end of his broadcasting career, apparently there were some difficulties and problems in the role he played there.

Romney Wheeler, Director of Public Relations for Consumers Power Company in Michigan, recalled meeting Murrow toward the end of the war.[1] Their paths crossed on a very occasional basis, when Wheeler was broadcasting for NBC and Murrow for CBS. In 1958, Wheeler became Director of International Television Services for the USIA, under the late George Allen. When Murrow took over the USIA in 1961, Wheeler reported to him for about a year before he returned to private industry.

Wheeler's comments on Murrow's role as an administrator were enlightening. He wrote:

> During that time, my relationship with Mr. Murrow could best be described as "arm's length." This is not to imply that there was any hostility or ill will; but simply that Mr. Murrow was rather a remote person who (in my opinion) did not communicate easily with his subordinates.
>
> He was a very creative person and---obviously---a very gifted journalist. However, as is the case with many creative and gifted people, he was not especially talented as an administrator.
>
> In my own working relationship with Mr. Murrow, I found that, while he had very decided views about what he wanted, he was unable to communicate them explicitly to me or my staff. This caused confusion and not a little frustration, because his criticisms and disagreements invariably came after the fact, rather than before. In short, we would have been delighted to produce a television program or film precisely to his specifications, if he could have given us those specifications beforehand.

Wheeler said that---with hindsight and the passing of years---he conceded that this difficulty would probably have arisen between any two people engaged in creative work in the same medium, such as television: "Mr. Murrow was a television professional and one who enjoyed a well-earned preeminence in his field. I also regarded myself as a professional in the same field.

Wheeler repeated that no two people in so highly individualistic a field as television would ever do a particular program in exactly the same manner. He continued:

> I think perhaps it comes back to the point I made about Mr. Murrow not being especially talented as an administrator. As Director of the USIA, he was required to be an administrator and a policy-maker. Yet, he was unable to separate that role from the creative role he had played so long in broadcasting.

---

[1] Romney Wheeler's comments about Edward R. Murrow are taken from a letter from him to the author dated September 21, 1971. Murrow first met Wheeler in London during the war when Wheeler broadcast for NBC.

Wheeler expanded and balanced his comments with the observations that Murrow was

> an outstanding personality . . . . a tremendously courageous man . . . tremendously gifted in communicating with millions of people by the medium of television.
> He had a deep social conscience and was a very troubled man. At the end, I think he also was saddened by his inability to change things to the better and (I suspect) was frustrated by the obstacles, difficulties and political maneuverings in Washington.

Wheeler's comments require some pondering. They are, perhaps, partially a key to understanding Murrow in his capacity as an administrator, and they may suggest another facet of his character. Wheeler concluded:

> Certainly he [Murrow] was a shy man in spite of being known to millions, and perhaps this was the crux of the problem. He could communicate effectively with the millions, but could not do so effectively with individuals.

It seems apparent that, as an administrator, Murrow was not a man for all seasons. Even his closest friends and colleagues of many years, Sevareid and Collingwood, reveal ambivalent reactions to Murrow in this capacity. Still, Wheeler's reactions are revealing in pointing to a quality within Murrow that made him more human and less the charismatic figure who related effectively to all. The thrust of most comments about Murrow in his dealings with others, however, were mainly complimentary about his interpersonal relationships with other colleagues and friends despite his administrative weaknesses.

It might be well to pause here and examine in some depth Murrow's general relationships with people and the ideas and values that he held dear, that do not relate to him in his role as administrator. This challenging but difficult piece of character analysis will be attempted in the next chapter.

CHAPTER XVI

"HE GRIPPED PEOPLE"

In London, Murrow was with people a great deal of the time. Early in the morning, on the streets, at the BBC, in R. T. Clark's office, in restaurants, in the Hallam Street flat, he was surrounded by people. They were, as we have gleaned, a source of news for him, a general sounding board for his ideas. He was genuinely but only generally concerned about people. Even those few whom he held in high regard were, in a sense, kept at "arm's length."

"He could absorb and reflect the thought and emotions of day laborers, airplane pilots, or cabinet ministers and report with exact truth what they were; yet he never gave an inch of himself away." That, at any rate, was how Eric Sevareid saw his colleague. His scripts and correspondence, the memos and reports in the BBC---these reflect not only a wide acquaintanceship with a diverse group of people, but Murrow's physical closeness to people as well.

On the subject of his interpersonal relationships, Charles Collingwood once observed:

>   Because of his remarkable personality, he had the most enormous range of contacts and friends among people of all walks of life, from the top on down.
>   Churchill conceived great regard for him. When Gil Winant was our ambassador here, he and Ed were very close. And as the British began to realize the impact of Murrow's broadcasts to the United States, they naturally were anxious to associate the U.S. with them in the war, more and more contacts were opened to him.
>   But they were of every kind; a radical like Harold Laski was an intimate friend of his, whereas the most conservative members of the government and the foreign office were also friends.
>   He had an enormous affinity with people. His house would always be full of bomber pilots on leave, or fighter pilots on leave, that he'd met. They'd come up to London, no hotel rooms---anyway, Ed wanted them to stay with him. He got onto good terms with people very quickly.

Collingwood also touched on Murrow's political inclinations: liberal, no doubt, but party was another question: "I don't suppose anyone could tell from his broadcasts whether he was a Democrat or a Republican. Or for whom he would be most likely to vote for President. He had friends in both camps."

Two such friends were decidedly at opposite ends of the traditional party structure. Collingwood recalls,

>   Harry Truman was a friend of his, and Ed much admired him. Tom Dewey was a neighbor of his in Pawling, New York. Ed

had the highest regard for Dewey. They used to play
golf together, talk politics together. It was the thing
itself that always interested Ed, and the human being
himself, rather than what flag he was under.

Replying to a 1959 inquiry, however, on what he knew about the relationship between Nixon and Dewey, Murrow replied, "My relations with Nixon are non-existent, and while Dewey and I are neighbors and friends, we have a sort of arm's-length relationship when it comes to politics."

And somewhat higher than any of these political figures was a man of letters. Poet Carl Sandburg was one of Murrow's personal heroes. When asked to write a brief tribute honoring Sandburg's seventy-fifth birthday, he wrote what was for him a long letter. (Murrow's correspondence was generally very brief, usually one succinct paragraph.) Murrow's admiration and love were quite evident. He wrote:

> It would require the eloquence of the ancients and Carl Sandburg to respond adequately to your request for some words of comment or tribute to Carl Sandburg.
> I have, by accident and by design, had occasion over the last twenty years to meet a not inconsiderable number of men whose names make headlines, as well as a few scholars and writers. It is part of a reporter's duty to be no man's disciple and to inoculate himself frequently against the disease known as hero-worship. So far as Sandburg is concerned I am a disciple with the disease and regard my lot as most fortunate.
> It would be possible, I imagine, for me to write at great length about this great man, but he would not approve for we both understand that "brevity is good both when you are and are not understood." Carl understands the depth and degree of my respect and affection for him, and he understands that I have insufficient command of the language for adequate expression.

In the area of race, we have come to regard segregation as harmful. Equally harmful is the process whereby we reinforce only our own views because we cling to "our kind." The pressures for so doing are often great in an urban society where we crave close affinities, where values are in flux and we need strength to maintain them. Murrow's habits of communication, formed during those war years in London, gave him a wider vision, a broader scope of people and events through his wide associations. He was better able to discover the nuances of a problem.

An active leader in the mass media once explained that limited and reinforcing relationships are a problem in trying to accomplish needed objectives. "Academics talk to academics in the quiet of their offices, secretaries to secretaries over coffee, and Rotarians to Rotarians." Integration is an ideal needed on all levels of society, and perhaps not easily obtainable.

It was clear to Eric Sevareid that Ed Murrow, though not yet thirty years old, was a natural leader: "It was extraordinary. Ed had a great gift for friendship, you know. That was one of his real gifts."

Like Michael Balkwill and Robert Reid, Sevareid emphasized that Murrow was not a volatile talker who dominated discussion. "He had power, a sense of authority about him. He didn't waste words much. He wasn't terribly loquacious." In fact, Sevareid said, people who talked a lot bored Murrow:

> Ed was a bad conversationalist, as a matter of fact. . . . He would tell stories occasionally. He had a sense of anecdotes.
> But . . . he'd sort of scowl and stare at the floor, and twist his thumbs, take a drag on a cigarette, listen, and then he'd make a kind of pronouncement.
> Not with many people did he have any sort of easy flow of conversation.

When asked about his reference to Murrow keeping a distance between himself and others, even those he loved, not revealing himself, Sevareid affirmed that such was the case: "Yes, I think he tended to hold people off at arm's length." But there was a case where he could really let down his hair, relax, and have a free and easy personal relationship:

> He loved Larry LeSeur a good deal, that summer of '40 and the following months of the blitz there. I was there part of that time. Larry was terribly easy-going and relaxed and funny, and he was good for Ed, I thought.
> No, I was a much more uptight sort of fellow, as they now say.

Ed liked people but recoiled from emotional outbursts, emphasized Sevareid: "He didn't like that. That embarrassed him." And his relationships with women were not easy. "He was very awkward about women. All kinds of attractive women, of course, were attracted to Ed. I think he was attracted to them, but he was very awkward about it; he didn't know how to speak to women."

When in the middle of an interview the author expressed mild surprise that Murrow could get on with world leaders but had difficulty relating to women, Sevareid interrupted:

> He was totally at ease with Winston Churchill, but let a beautiful show girl or actress come up to him and he'd be pretty inarticulate. And I think he stayed that way. I don't think he ever had a sense of ease with beautiful women that he sensed were interested in him.

Sevareid recalled occasions when Murrow was discernably moved by his own broadcasts: "I think sometimes just the sheer power of his own words, figures of speech, would slightly overcome him, too. Because they were powerful. They were eloquent." He added that he didn't think Murrow knew, for a long time, the effect that he was having in America. Sevareid came home in November of 1940, after spending the summer after the fall of France with Murrow in London. "And I didn't realize it---it suddenly hit me when I got here. The whole damn country was listening to us every day! Ed was having a monumental international effect!

"He simply gripped people!"

CHAPTER XVII

"THIS I BELIEVE"

Much that we have noted so far in Murrow's behavior depicts what he believed and what was important to him. Reading his scripts from throughout the years that he was involved in the field of broadcast journalism reveals the same values. The values he lived by, in other words, were the same values that shaped his radio and television personality and influenced the content of his messages.

In Ed Murrow's life and acts, it was evident that he valued the sanctity of the individual person. He was a humanist. Anything that threatened the right of the individual to fulfill himself, to grow in freedom, was his sworn enemy. Thus it was that fascism topped his list of world evils because it was antithetical to his respect for the individual person.

Did this philosophy come from his North Carolina childhood, or from his labors in the Washington forests where he learned the rigors of work and team effort? Did it first arise at Washington State University where debate, dramatics, and campus leadership taught him the values of individual creativity and thinking? Or did it come from travel, or work with the Institute of International Education? His meetings with expatriate German professors obviously contributed, as did his experiences in Vienna and, of course, in London. The whole of his life's value system came into play---not only when Adolf Hitler came to power, for example, but whenever the individual was a victim, whether of a senatorial demagogue or a system that deprived certain groups of such basic rights that all that was reaped was a "harvest of shame."

Edward R. Murrow had a philosophical kinship to the long libertarian tradition of England. Locke, Harrington, Mill, Paine, and Jefferson (along with Marcus Aurelius) were companions of his mind. Rather than teaching on a formal basis, Murrow would instead write, and be where the action was when the times and situations demanded. Yet in the broadest sense, he was a teacher, and each broadcast was a learning experience for his listeners.

We have only to return to the end of the war years, to the time when "A Reporter Remembers" and says farewell to a land that had become his home for nearly a decade to understand his basic philosophy. What had the war really meant? He told us, and very briefly. Not bravery and courage, though he had seen both. Not dedication nor service, though weary men had given both. What Ed Murrow thought was this: "I am persuaded that the most important thing that happened in Britain was that this nation chose to win or lose this war under the established rules of parliamentary procedure." The rule of law that protected the individual: that was the real victor in this war, because it was held paramount in a nation under siege, a hair's-breadth away from destruction by a totalitarian enemy.

"Do you remember," he asked, "that while London was being bombed in the daylight, the House devoted two days to discussing conditions under which enemy aliens were detained on the Isle of Man? Though Britain fell, there were to be no concentration camps here. . . . There was still law in the land, regardless of race, nationality or hatred. Representative government, equality before the law, survived."

He was satisfied, it seemed. He would go home, but he noted that "I have been privileged to see an entire people give the reply to tyranny that their history demanded of them."

Earlier, as war raged around the world, Murrow and his friend Harold Laski discussed the subject of education on one of the BBC "Freedom Forum" programs. The topic was public education and its ability to equip the citizen for his postwar task. In the discussion, Murrow showed that he had not forgotten his roots:

> It seems to me that equality of educational opportunity is clear enough. In my own country, for instance, children down in some of the poorer Southern states receive only four months of schooling every year. Their teachers are poorly trained and the libraries are inadequate, and it seems to some of us that it's unfair that a child should be so penalized just because he happens to have been born in Mississippi or in Louisiana, rather than in one of the richer states . . . in New York or California, for instance.

When Laski suggested, that, no matter what one's profession or job, he had to have the knowledge, the education to be able to choose his rulers and hold them to account, Murrow answered, "It seems to me that Laski has exactly stated the American philosophy of higher education." But Murrow, thirty years ago, did not hold higher education to be a panacea for all problems in a democracy: "I think you'd agree, Harold, that it's possible at least that in America we place too much emphasis upon higher education and we've come to have a sort of unquestioning belief in the efficiency of it."

When he was asked about the status of the teacher in America, Murrow felt that there had been a change for the better: "A great deal of that change has been brought about in the course of the last ten years. College professors, for instance, have been made almost respectable, because the New Deal brought them down to Washington, and state and municipal administrations followed suit and people became convinced that those professors really knew something." Some years later, Murrow joined Kennedy's administration, which like Franklin Roosevelt's sought to bring a "brain trust" to Washington to cope with a multitude of social and economic problems.

In his discussion with Laski, Murrow continued with a curious word of thanks to the Fuehrer: "My great educational debt is to Hitler . . . the best education I ever received came from German professors who were flung out of German universities by Hitler."

When the topic switched to English education, another panel participant, George Young, suggested that perhaps the outstanding quality of British education was "considerateness." Murrow wanted an amendment: "Considerateness . . . it's always seemed to me that perhaps tolerance expressed it a little better, and I have the belief that that's the one thing that British education at its best has to teach." But he added a warning: "It's possible for that tolerance to cross over the narrow borderline into . . . smugness, complacency, indifference---whatever you like."

In concluding the program, Ed Murrow, the man of action, wanted only this: greater communication and understanding among men. "I should like to see . . . a Lend-Lease Act that applied to professors, in order that we might exchange, between my own country and Britain, more professors." Murrow was prepared, had he the power, to trade several squadrons of aircraft and a raft of tanks, "if we might have Laski and Young in the States for a few years after this is all over."

A week earlier in the same program Murrow had made the point that the emphasis in higher education should be on responsibility, not on privilege. However, it seemed to Murrow that the latter was precisely the direction that higher education was taking:

> Higher education, perhaps throughout the whole English-speaking world, and particularly in the States, has tended more and more to produce graduates with a sense of privilege rather than a sense of responsibility. The objective seems to have been personal profit at the expense of the society that's made possible superior intellectual training for a relatively small number.
>
> And it seems to me that if postwar education is to produce useful leaders . . . we must place the emphasis upon responsibility rather than privilege.

What would Murrow have thought about higher education as exemplified by anti-Vietnam war demonstrations and protest rallies on college campuses that developed shortly after his death? Were not things now turned around? Was there an emphasis not on greed or special privilege, but on concern for others, for improving society, for accepting and promoting responsible actions? Or would he have considered the protest rallies a threat to an orderly democratic system?

Of course, we do not know. But one man has a strong idea about what Murrow would have thought. Murrow may have held a high regard for, and concern about, the role of higher education, but according to Eric Sevareid, "There are many things being said and done today he'd have been indignant about." He emphasized that Murrow never fell into "academic liberalism." Sevareid elaborated:

> Well, look, at that time . . . the Depression years, for example, and the war years; the liberal writing and theater, Clifford Odets and what not, was a very genuine thing.

A really generous and compassionate kind of intellectual . . . truly concerned over the physical condition and every other condition of unfortunate, down-trodden people. And there were a hell of a lot more of them then than there are now.

This theater of today, take that example, dealing with the blacks and poor and what not, is far more the theater of self-pity.

It's the intellectuals pitying themselves. It's the whole ingrown self-examination. Norman Mailer is a great example, but he happens to have a kind of genius, it's readable . . . you're interested in the condition of his soul.

This now has infected everything, including reporters on big papers. Got to tell you the condition of their soul before they tell you what happened.

Ed wouldn't have stood for that, I don't think. That's the difference.

There's a sickliness about a lot of this compassion. Especially from academic liberals. Because they're all middle-class people who don't know what working people are like, or what the people in the black ghetto really want. At the same time they want to uplift them; at the same time they hate the middle class.

Well, there's no place for them to go but the middle class. That's been the name of the game for a thousand years. Try to have a piece of land, a little sky over you, a good roof for your children, what the hell's it been about *except* this, on a material level?

At the same time, that's all despised by them, the middle class, so what in the hell do they want? Become a revolutionary? There isn't going to be any revolution.

And I think Ed would have had little time for this.

Sevareid referred to Vietnam, and compared that war with the Spanish Civil War. First off, Sevareid conceded that there were "certainly differences between Vietnam and the Spanish Civil War; but in the Spanish Civil War," he pointed out, "the left-wing idealists here, who hated fascism, went there by the hundreds and were killed and fought."

Sevareid said that he had yet to know of a single Weatherman, or a young American who was pro-Ho Chi Minh, who had gone to North Vietnam and fought for them:

It's difficult, it's different, because we're involved directly in this country. But even so, I think there's a certain point in that comparison.

Now this is talk, this is posturing, so much of it. That was life and death, you know. Ed knew what life and death were, he knew what real poverty was. Very poor. A lot of what's happening with some of these kids would not have amused him.

Sevareid, in pushing his points home, made his interpretation clear. Murrow did indeed want higher education to have responsibility, social and personal concern, and an ethical base. But it had to be real.

What of civil rights? Murrow in the 1940's would hardly have qualified as leading the vanguard of racial understanding and awareness as we attempt to understand such complexities today. Yes, he believed in equality. But he was a victim of his own background and---if we can judge by what he said---relatively unaware of the dimensions of racism, of black contributions to America, of the black presence and thought in our culture. Even the contradiction involved in the completely segregated American forces during World War II fighting a "holy" war against Hitlerian tyranny and racism appeared to go unnoticed by Murrow and his media colleagues.

On one BBC program in 1942, for example, called "Books That Made History," Murrow discussed *Uncle Tom's Cabin*. It was a twenty-minute broadcast, and his Southern background and attitude came through in his Home Service talk, as well as his usual identifiable desire to communicate rather than inflame:

> By the 1850's, slavery was on the way out anyway. We needn't have fought a war over it. . . . Slavery would have ended without the impetus of the Civil War, had the Northerners not raised such a hue and cry about the immorality of the system.
>
> The Southerners being mainly Anglo-Saxon stock wouldn't stand for that, and they rose in defense of their system.

And he made a statement that, in the context of the 1970's, would be entirely out of place in speaking of the blacks under slavery: "They were well cared for generally. They lived under a feudal system. . . . Of course, there were abuses."

There is a "peculiar institution" kind of acceptance of slavery in the statement: the "darkies" were basically "happy out back," although a few abuses existed. There was no real condemnation of the system itself.

Murrow went on to say that the book *Uncle Tom's Cabin* did not start the Civil War, despite President Lincoln's compliment to Harriet Beecher Stowe, but was an "inflamatory document" which did create a great deal of hatred and bitterness. He said that the author had very little firsthand information about conditions in the South, and he said "the book is not to be read as an accurate portrayal of slave life in the Southern states."

Murrow concluded: "Those who defended slavery with their lives, and those who fought against it, now agree that American slavery was on the whole a humane and civilized institution compared with the present practices of the Germans."

In the context of the general ignorance in Britain concerning the history of American slavery, the temper of the times, and the genocidal butchering by the Nazis, perhaps the statement could stand up. To the black man who inherited the legacy of this "peculiar institution"---living in squalor in the ghettos of our large cities, "a humane and civilized institution" has a very hollow ring. Is all this recorded here to "expose" Murrow's blind side, or to debunk his humanistic bent? Not so. It is recorded to reflect a part of the man, and his own human ability to be caught in the web of his upbringing and education, of the socialization process that tended to condition his thinking later in life, as it does with all of us.

His concepts and values relating to black history in America, and his ideas on Harriet Beecher Stowe's book were no different from those of most socially concerned persons of that day. For, in 1942, there was simply a general ignoring of, and ignorance about, the plight of the black man in America. This situation was made clear to the British people when large numbers of American troops began to arrive in England in 1942 and 1943, with all troop units completely segregated by race and color.

Murrow's interpretation of history regarding slavery may have been askew, but not his values. In an earlier broadcast to the British, for example, he had commented: "When certain sections of our press give you advice about India, remember that it's easier to urge freedom and equality for people thousands of miles away than it is to provide it for our Negroes here at home."

Murrow's later powerful documentary on poverty, "Harvest of Shame," was one of his last pieces of professional and commercial journalism completed before he joined the United States Information Agency. Leonard Miall of the BBC recalled vividly an incident that happened regarding the "Harvest of Shame" broadcast.

The subject arose as a result of an interview with Miall when a question about Murrow's religious attitudes---whether Miall thought that Murrow was religious in any formal sense---arose. He replied, "I would think not, but I would think it [Murrow's personal religious conviction] was very deep down." Something in that brief discussion led him to think of "Harvest of Shame." Miall recalled being in charge of BBC's current and public affairs programs for television at the time the "incident" occurred. The BBC had used much of Murrow's material, Miall commented, including programs from the "Small World" and "See It Now" series. Then he referred specifically to the "Harvest of Shame" broadcast:

> One of the first things he [Murrow] had to do at Kennedy's request, because he was needing the support of certain Southern senators on something or other, was to try to ring up the BBC and prevent us from broadcasting this.

The BBC, of course, refused. And what was Murrow's reaction? Miall added:

> I think he was enormously relieved when we refused to cancel it.
> I was involved in this. He actually rang up Hugh Green who was the Director General, but I was the man in charge of the Department that was putting it on. Hugh Green was talking to me about it.

Green had told him that he wouldn't dream of taking it off, and I think [Murrow] was relieved, and subsequently slightly ashamed that he asked us to. Particularly as this was one of the first things he had to do as the Director of USIA.

Others who had worked closely with Murrow had additional comments in reply to questions concerning Murrow's beliefs and values. Frank Gillard, for example, expressed what he thought Murrow's values were in a series of abstractions: "goodness, truth, beauty, fairness, impartiality, sense of taste, sense of purpose."

Charles Collingwood seemed to feel that there was only one way to put it:

Well, you know, one gets into all these big generalizations. But besides the truth, which to him was a constant object of pursuit, there are things that sound awfully big and windy, but things like honor---very important to him---his personal honor, his country's honor, and concepts like that made his heart beat faster.

Eric Sevareid in commenting on the same question concerning Murrow said,

He was a great moralist, you know. He expected individuals, and his government, to live up to high moral standards. He believed in a kind of foreign policy based, I think, on that, on moral principles, which few people really believe in anymore.

When asked what one thing, one value, seemed to permeate Murrow's character, Sevareid replied quickly, with one word: "Decency." He explained:

I don't mean that in a puritanical sense. He couldn't stand people who pushed other people around. He just loathed people who abused power, abused weak people, took advantage of those who couldn't answer back. He couldn't stand that.

When asked if that comment applied, "Whether it was McCarthy or Hitler?", Sevareid shot back: "McCarthy, Hitler, whoever the hell it was. He just felt that was indecent."

Over and over again, in comments from colleagues and friends, there seemed to be a unanimity of opinion about what, in the last analysis, mattered to Edward R. Murrow. The individual. The individual person. People. The little people.

Sevareid thought it was his upbringing, his personal experience:

Ed had a real feeling, you see, about working-class people, the poor, the farmers; he'd done a lot of that.

> Again, that was so much my background. We both came from kind of middle-class families in a way, we had gone through the Depression . . . a lot of poverty in our families. We both had to work like dogs---farm work and every other kind of damfool thing. . . . He had a feeling about this!

As the war moved into its final phases, Murrow again expressed his personal feelings on a special "Freedom Forum" program. With him on the program were Sir Frederick Whyte, his friend Harold Laski, and Conservative Henry Brooke, Member of Parliament. It was shortly before the invasion, and the topic of the program concerned the possibility of achieving a classless society in the postwar world. Murrow started the discussion by stating:

> From what I have seen here in the last four years, I have come to the conclusion that in general the aristocrats in this country are the people who work with their hands, who have grease under the fingernails.
> I conclude that because, during the blitz, they were the toughest citizens that I've ever seen, and took their bombing, I think, on the whole much better than the people who were in higher estate.

As to materialistic values, Murrow, being human, liked the "good things of life" as these are generally understood, but it was rather obvious---as well as generally expressed---that material comforts were not high on his list of priorities.

As Sir Lindsay Wellington put it, he was "entirely unmoved, I would think, by money." Sir Lindsay felt that Murrow was never impressed by the fact that someone was very rich or lofty: "Oh, he'd be well mannered and respectful to the President or Prime Minister. He wasn't prepared to give up his basic thinking for that reason alone."

Godfrey Talbot, who saw much of Murrow when England was being bombarded, said, "There was nothing else tugging at him . . . to do other things . . . go and play golf." Covering the story, the pursuit of the news: "This was life, and this was what he wanted to devote his whole life to, as far as I could see." As to the material blessings of his existence? "I'm not suggesting that Ed Murrow didn't like food and drink and good company. Of course he did. My goodness, he did," Talbot emphasized. "But the hour of the day didn't matter, if there was some information to be got, some new human being to meet, this was what mattered. Not food; not drink; not going to sleep."

The social and ethical values of Murrow, Sir Lindsay felt, "all lay along the line of compassion, of a sense of fairness and justice, a dislike of oppression."

Michael Standing called it "justice." For him, Murrow was obviously greatly concerned with justice.

But always it was people . . . people . . . people. From that perspective it is revealing to look at some of the ways that people who knew him best described his value system---

Sir Lindsay Wellington: He had, of course, a great admiration for Churchill; how he was using words, bringing people together, showing them the light at the end of the tunnel. But basically he was more devoted to the common man.

Michael Standing: He was obviously greatly concerned with the common people, not common in the perjorative sense---I mean the general run of people, having a decent life, being able to draw the real advantages from the philosophies of people cleverer than themselves.
 I think he was a tremendous champion of the bravery of people, the good qualities that the war brought out. I think he greatly admired the general reaction of people here to the blitz, the old people, helpless people who were being bombed, who had their homes destroyed, who had their relatives killed . . . the resilience of people.
 I think he saw in this the great hope for the future; that people could respond in this way.

Godfrey Talbot: What mattered to Ed Murrow, I think, was not what you were in status---whether you were the chief of a department, or a town clerk, or a manager, or a general. What mattered was whether you, first of all, were a genuine person.

Murrow didn't have time for people who were pompous, Talbot said, people who were putting on an act or talking for talking's sake. "What he did have time for were human beings of all kinds, of all walks, who were straightforward, who had experience of all sorts of things; he had a sharp nose for phonies. What mattered to him, I think, was human endeavor, fun; not what is regarded as fun nowadays---discotheques, frothy humor---though he had a tremendous sense of humor."

Robert Reid: The only thing that mattered were people---how they lived and worked, what chances they had in life. A very tolerant man where toleration was needed, with a belief in equal opportunity, and a man who could stand up and fight for those things. He wasn't a weak man.

Michael Balkwill: He was interested, it seemed to me, in people, in talking with people, in books that had been written, in conversations---talking, thinking, reading--- rather than a go-getting journalist out to get a scoop, make a pile, or make the headlines.

That wasn't in his make-up, said Balkwill. But people were. "He had a great regard for people . . . not in any clinical way or, least of all, in any patronizing way. He was interested in communication. I suppose this would be the key to it."

And, finally, there was Mary Adams. She volunteered the comment that "he had a set of values which persisted."

When I asked, "What set of values?", she placed her cup of tea on the saucer with great dignity, leaned back on the sofa in the small room of the Royal Society for the Arts on John Adam Street, and replied, "People mattered." For Edward R. Murrow, we might take the liberty of posthumously adding his favorite postscript to Mary Adams comment---"This I believe."

SELECTED READINGS

Bliss, Edward, Jr., ed. *In Search of Light---The Broadcasts of Edward R. Murrow 1938-1969.* New York: Alfred A. Knopf, 1967.

Bridson, D. G. *Prospero and Ariel, The Rise and Fall of Radio---A Personal Recollection.* London: Victor Gollancz Ltd., 1971.

Briggs, Asa. *The War of Words---The History of Broadcasting in the United Kingdom,* Volume III. London: Oxford University Press, 1970.

Kendrick, Alexander. *Prime Time---The Life of Edward R. Murrow.* Boston: Little, Brown, 1969.

Miall, Leonard, ed. *Richard Dimbleby, Broadcaster.* London: British Broadcasting Corporation, 1966.

Morgan, Edward P., ed. *This I Believe.* New York: Simon and Schuster, 1952.

Murrow, Edward R. (ed. by Elmer Davis). *This is London.* New York: Simon and Schuster, 1941.

Sevareid, Eric. *Not So Wild a Dream.* New York: Alfred A. Knopf, 1947.

APPENDIX A

INTERVIEWS

The following individuals were interviewed by the author personally or by letter, on the dates and at the places indicated. The substance of the book is based mainly on the interviews and other communications received from former colleagues of Edward R. Murrow. These are the people who are best able to describe and evaluate Murrow's contributions to the field of broadcast journalism. He had a close working association and personal relationship with many of them. Their comments about Edward R. Murrow, taken from these interviews for the most part, are sprinkled throughout the book and provide an element of authenticity and credibility that library research alone could not possibly have offered. The author has intended through the selection process to give the reader a balanced view of the man, his ideas, and his actions.

Mary Adams   Interviewed on Wednesday, June 23, 1971, at the Royal Society for the Arts on John Adam Street, London.

                   Mary Adams was a biologist in the 1920's, a geneticist with a special interest in heredity. She began her radio career by giving talks over the BBC on these and other scientific subjects. In 1930 she joined the BBC in charge of current affairs, focusing mainly on scientific programs. In 1936 she moved to BBC-TV and in 1939 she accepted a position with the Ministry of Information in the Home Intelligence Branch. She later returned to the BBC and was in charge of Talks and Documentaries.

Herbert Agar   Letter dated June 5, 1971, received in response to specific interview questions submitted to him by the author.

                   Henry Agar was an American newspaper correspondent and editor. From 1942 to 1946 he was Special Assistant to the American Ambassador in London. He also served as President of Freedom House in New York from 1941 to 1943.

Michael Balkwill   Interviewed on Monday, May 10, 1971, in the BBC Club.

                   Michael Balkwill joined the BBC in 1933 as a junior in the newsroom. Starting as a junior-sub-editor, he was later made duty editor putting him in immediate charge of preparation of bulletins throughout the day. He performed these kinds of functions during the war period, and, after the war, was transferred to BBC-TV in 1950.

Thomas Barman

Interviewed on Wednesday, April 7, 1971, at the Devonshire Club in London.

Before the war, Thomas Barman was a member of the foreign staff of the *London Times*, covering the Low Countries, Scandinavia, and France. From 1939 to 1942 he served in the Enemy Propaganda Department and from 1943 to 1945 he was personal assistant to the British Ambassador in Moscow. In 1946 he joined the BBC and served as a diplomatic correspondent, covering diplomatic news in London and elsewhere.

Robert Barr

Interviewed on Monday, May 10, 1971, at the BBC Club.

Robert Barr served as a BBC Correspondent during the war period.

I. D. Benzie

Interviewed on Friday, June 25, 1971, at her flat in London.

I. D. Benzie joined the BBC in 1927 and served as Secretary to the Foreign Director. In 1931 she became Foreign Director.

D. G. Bridson

Interviewed on Friday, May 21, 1971, at the Saville Club, and on Friday, May 28, 1971, at Bridson's home.

D. G. Bridson joined the BBC in 1935 and served with the Corporation until 1969. He first met Edward R. Murrow in 1941. He served as a writer and producer for the BBC in the five years preceding the war, then helped to run the documentary section. In the latter position he wrote many documentaries for American consumption concerning the British war effort. He noted that he "kept running across Ed while gathering material" for these documentaries.

Charles Collingwood	Interviewed on Wednesday, April 7, 1971, at CBS headquarters in London.
	Charles Collingwood joined CBS as News Commentator in the early months of 1941 after having served with United Press as a War Correspondent in London from 1939 to 1941. He worked for Ed Murrow and CBS in London until the end of the war. Currently he continues to work for CBS as a Foreign Correspondent and News Analyst.
Charles Curran	Letter received dated December 18, 1969, containing references to BBC associates who had known or worked with Edward R. Murrow.
	Sir Charles Curran served in the Indian Army from 1941 to 1945. Returning to Britain at the war's end, he became Producer of Home Talks with the BBC in 1947. After a long career, he became Director-General of the BBC in 1969.
Robin Duff	Interviewed on Friday, April 16, 1971, at his home Meldrum House in Old Meldrum, Aberdeenshire, Scotland.
	Robin Duff joined the BBC in 1937 and served as Chief Reporter. He was a BBC Correspondent at the war's end. He had a close association with Edward R. Murrow in London throughout the war period.
Robert Dunnett	Interviewed on Saturday, April 17, 1971, at his home in Edinburgh, Scotland.
	Robert Dunnett joined the BBC in the mid-1930's and served as a BBC Correspondent during the war years.
Frank Gillard	Letter dated July 21, 1970, received by the author in response to questions concerning Edward R. Murrow's London career.
	Frank Gillard served as a freelance broadcaster from 1936 until he joined the BBC as Talks Producer in 1941. In 1941 he was appointed BBC War Correspondent and served in that position until the war's end.

Cecilia Reeves (Mrs. Darsie Gillie)	Interviewed in two telephone conversations and in a letter dated May 29, 1971, received by the author.
	Cecilia Reeves served with the BBC during the war period. She was a personal acquaintance of Edward R. Murrow during that era.
Maurice Gorham	Letter dated May 24, 1971, received in response to interview questions.
	Maurice Gorham played an important role in BBC operations during the war period. Comments by Gorham about Edward R. Murrow found in the book are taken from the letter noted above.
Noel Harvey	Although no formal interview was conducted, the author had many useful conversations with him about the wartime conditions and personalities involved in BBC operations.
	Noel Harvey served as Overseas Liaison Officer and as Head of Liaison, Overseas and Foreign Relations of the BBC at Broadcasting House in London.
Pierre LeFevre	Letter dated April 13, 1971, received by the author.
	Pierre LeFevre served as a BBC Correspondent during the war period.
Richard Marriott	Interviewed on Tuesday, June 1, 1971, at Marriott's home in Hampstead, England.
	Richard Marriott began his career with the BBC in 1933 as an announcer and in 1935 joined the Foreign Department, serving both NBC and CBS networks.
	In 1939 at the outbreak of the war he created a BBC Monitoring Unit and served in France. After returning and serving with the BBC in London, he joined the RAF Fighter Command in 1942 and served out the war as a navigator. After the war, he rejoined the BBC and served in several capacities.

Howard Marshall	Letter dated March 25, 1971, in response to author's request for information.
	Howard Marshall served as a BBC Correspondent during the war period.
Leonard Miall	Interviewed on Wednesday, April 14, 1971, in Miall's office at Broadcast House. In addition, a large number of letters were exchanged between Leonard Miall and the author relating to Edward R. Murrow and his wartime career.
	Leonard Miall joined the BBC in 1939 and inaugurated talks broadcasts to Europe that year. From 1940 to 1942 he served as German Talks and Features Editor, and from 1942 to 1944 he was a member of the British Political Warfare Mission to the United States. In 1944 he served with Political Warfare and in 1944 he was attached to the Psychological Warfare Division of SHAEF in Luxembourg. In 1945 he rejoined the BBC as Special Correspondent assigned to Czechoslovakia. Since the end of World War II, Leonard Miall has held many important posts with the BBC, spending much of that period in the United States.
Royston Morley	Interviewed on Wednesday, June 23, 1971, at Morley's office in Hanover Square. Also a number of letters were exchanged between Morley and the author.
	Royston Morley was associated with BBC-TV during its early period of operations. He got to know Edward R. Murrow during the latter part of the 1930's.
Robert Reid	Interviewed on Friday, April 23, 1971, at Reid's home in Royal Tunbridge Wells, Kent.
	Robert Reid was a Correspondent with the BBC during the war period. He joined the BBC a fortnight before war broke out in 1939. After the war, Reid worked with the BBC and also as a newspaper writer.
Eric Sevareid	Interviewed on Tuesday, August 3, 1971, in Sevareid's office at CBS in Washington, D.C.
	Eric Sevareid has been a leading radio and television correspondent and analyst for over

thirty-five years. He began his career as a newspaper reporter and editor, and, while serving as Night Editor of the United Press in Paris in 1939 he was hired by Edward R. Murrow as European Correspondent for CBS. He is the author of several books that deal with his association with Edward R. Murrow during and after the war years.

Colston Shepherd   Letter dated April 8, 1971, received by the author in response to questions concerning Edward R. Murrow's activities during the war years.

Colston Shepherd was Secretary-General of the Air League of the British Empire from 1944 to 1950. In 1944 he was seconded to serve with the BBC as War Correspondent with the RAF.

Patrick Smith   Letter dated May 7, 1971, received by the author in response to questions concerning Edward R. Murrow's activities during the war years.

Patrick Smith served as a War Correspondent with the BBC during the war period.

Michael Standing   Interviewed on Thursday, April 8, 1971, at Standing's home in Borough Green, Kent.

Michael Standing joined the BBC in 1935. From 1940 to 1945, he was BBC Director of Outside Broadcasting.

Godfrey Talbot   Interviewed on Thursday, April 22, 1971, at Broadcast House in London.

Godfrey Talbot joined the BBC in 1937 after a ten-year career as a newspaperman and editor. He served as a BBC War Correspondent overseas from 1941 to 1945. After the war he continued to pursue a successful career as author, broadcaster, lecturer, journalist and Commentator on the BBC staff.

Eric Warr   Letter dated June 25, 1971, received by the author in response to questions concerning Edward R. Murrow's activities during the war years.

	Eric Warr served in various capacities with the BBC during the war period.
Lindsay Wellington	Interviewed on Wednesday, March 17, 1971, by the author at Wellington's home in Henley-on-Thames, Oxfordshire.
	Sir Lindsay Wellington began his long career with the BBC in 1924 when he joined the BBC Programme Staff. In 1940 he was appointed Director of the Broadcasting Division of the Ministry of Information. From 1941 to 1944, Sir Lindsay served as North American Director of BBC operations. He retired from the BBC in 1963 after a distinguished career.
Romney Wheeler	Letter dated September 21, 1971, received by the author in response to questions concerning Edward R. Murrow's career.
	Romney Wheeler first met Edward R. Murrow in London near the end of the war, when he was working for NBC and Ed was with CBS. When Murrow was appointed Director of the United States Information Agency in 1961, Wheeler as Director of International Television Services reported to him.